SCHAUM'S

BOOKKEEPING
AND ACCOUNTING

Other Books in Schaum's Easy Outlines Series Include:

SCHAUM'S *Easy* OUTLINES

BOOKKEEPING AND ACCOUNTING

BASED ON SCHAUM'S
Outline of Theory and Problems of
Bookkeeping and Accounting, Third Edition
BY JOEL J. LERNER, M.S., Ph.D.

ABRIDGEMENT EDITORS
DANIEL L. FULKS, Ph.D.
AND
MICHAEL K. STATON

SCHAUM'S OUTLINE SERIES

McGRAW-HILL

New York   Chicago   San Francisco   Lisbon   London   Madrid
Mexico City   Milan   New Delhi   San Juan
Seoul   Singapore   Sydney   Toronto

The McGraw·Hill Companies

JOEL J. LERNER is retired Professor and former Chairman of the business division at Sullivan County Community College in New York. He received his B.S. from New York University and his M.S. and Ph.D. degrees from Columbia University. He has written several *Schaum's Outlines* and lectures widely on finance.

DANIEL L. FULKS is Associate Professor and Director of the Accounting Program at Transylvania University in Lexington, Kentucky. He received a B.S. degree from the University of Tennessee, an M.B.A. from the University of Maryland, and a Ph.D. from Georgia State University. He is also a Certified Public Accountant. He taught previously at the University of Kentucky and worked in private business for several years. He is the abridgement editor for *Schaum's Easy Outline: Principles of Accounting* and co-editor for *Schaum's Easy Outline: Business Statistics*.

MICHAEL K. STATON is an associate with the accounting firm KPMG LLP in Denver, Colorado. He received a B.A. degree in accounting from Transylvania University in Lexington, Kentucky, and an M.T. from the University of Denver. He is the co-abridgement editor for *Schaum's Easy Outline: Business Statistics*.

Library of Congress Cataloging-in-Publication Data applied for.

5 6 7 8 9 0   FGR FGR 0 9 8 7

ISBN 0-07-142240-4

Contents

Chapter 1
ASSETS, LIABILITIES, AND CAPITAL

IN THIS CHAPTER:

- ✔ *Nature of Accounting*
- ✔ *Basic Elements of Financial Position: The Accounting Equation*
- ✔ *Summary*
- ✔ *Solved Problems*

Nature of Accounting

An understanding of the principles of book-keeping and accounting is essential for anyone who is interested in a successful career in business. The purpose of bookkeeping and accounting is to provide information concerning the financial affairs of a business. This information is needed by owners, managers, creditors, and governmental agencies.

An individual who earns a living by recording the financial activities of a business is known as a *bookkeeper,* while the process of classifying and summarizing business transactions and interpreting their effects is accomplished by the *accountant*. The bookkeeper is concerned with techniques involving the recording transactions, and the accountant's objective is the use of data for interpretation. Bookkeeping and accounting techniques will both be discussed.

Basic Elements of Financial Position: The Accounting Equation

The financial condition or position of a business enterprise is represented by the relationship of assets to liabilities and capital.

Assets: Properties that are owned and have money value—for instance, cash, inventory, buildings, equipment.

Liabilities: Amounts owed to outsiders, such as notes payable, accounts payable, bonds payable.

Capital: The interest of the owners in an enterprise; also known as owners' equity.

These three basic elements are connected by a fundamental relationship called *the accounting equation*. This equation expresses the equality of the assets on one side with the claims of the creditors and owners on the other side:

Assets = Liabilities + Owner's Equity

REMEMBER

The accounting equation of Assets = Liabilities + Owner's Equity should balance after every transaction.

Example 1.1

During the month of January, Mr. Patrick Incitti, lawyer,

1. Invested $5,000 to open his law practice.
2. Bought office supplies on account, $500.
3. Received $2,000 in fees earned during the month.
4. Paid $100 on the account for the office supplies.
5. Withdrew $500 for personal use.

These transactions could be analyzed and recorded as follows:

	Assets	=	**Liabilities**	+	**Capital**
	Cash				Incitti, Capital
1.	+ $5,000	=			+ $5,000
	Supplies		Accounts Payable		
2.	+ $500	=	+ $500		
	Cash				
3.	+ $2,000	=			Fees Income
	Cash				+ $2,000
4.	− $100	=	Accounts Payable		
	Cash		− $100		
5.	− $500	=			Incitti, Capital
					− $500

Notice that for every transaction, two entries are made. After every transaction, the accounting equation remains balanced.

Summary

1. The accounting equation is _____ = _____ + _____.
2. Items owned by a business that have monetary value are _____.
3. _____ is the interest of the owners in a business.
4. Money owed to an outsider is a(n) _____.
5. The difference between assets and liabilities is _____.
6. An investment in the business increases _____ and _____.
7. To purchase "on account" is to create a _____.

Answers: 1. Assets, liabilities, capital; 2. Assets; 3. Capital; 4. Liability; 5. Capital; 6. Assets, capital; 7. Liability

Solved Problems

Solved Problem 1.1 Given any two known elements, the third can easily be computed. Determine the missing amount in each of the accounting equations below.

	Assets	=	Liabilities	+	Capital
(a)	$7,200	=	$2,800	+	?
(b)	7,000	=	?	+	$4,400
(c)	?	=	2,000	+	4,400
(d)	20,000	=	5,600	+	?

Solution:

	Assets	=	Liabilities	+	Capital
(a)	$7,200	=	$2,800	+	$4,400
(b)	7,000	=	2,600	+	$4,400
(c)	6,400	=	2,000	+	4,400
(d)	20,000	=	5,600	+	14,400

Solved Problem 1.2 Classify each of the following as elements of the accounting equation using the following abbreviations: A = Assets; L = Liabilities; C = Capital

    (a) Land
    (b) Accounts Payable
    (c) Owners' Investment
    (d) Accounts Receivable

Solution:

(a) A; (b) L; (c) C; (d) A

Solved Problem 1.3 Determine the effect of the following transactions on capital.

    (a)   Bought machinery on account.
    (b)   Paid the above bill.
    (c)   Withdrew money for personal use.
    (d)   Inventory of supplies decreased by the end of the month.

Solution:

    (a)   No effect—only the asset and liability are affected.
    (b)   No effect same reason.
    (c)   Decrease in capital—capital is withdrawn.
    (d)   Decrease in capital—supplies that are used represent an expense.

Chapter 2
DEBITS AND CREDITS: THE DOUBLE-ENTRY SYSTEM

Introduction

Preparing a new equation $A = L + C$ after each transaction would be cumbersome and costly, especially when there are a great many transactions in an accounting period. Also, information for a specific item

6

such as cash would be lost as successive transactions were recorded. This information could be obtained by going back and summarizing the transactions, but that would be very time-consuming. Thus we begin with the *account.*

The Account

An account may be defined as *a record of the increases, decreases, and balances in an individual item of asset, liability, capital, income (revenue), or expense.*

The simplest form of the account is known as the "T" account because it resembles the letter "T." The account has three parts:

1. the name of the account and the account number
2. the debit side (left side), and
3. the credit side (right side).

The increases are entered on one side, the decreases on the other. The balance (the excess of the total of one side over the total of the other) is inserted near the last figure on the side with the larger amount.

Debits and Credits

When an amount is entered on the left side of an account, it is a debit, and the account is said to be *debited.* When an amount is entered on the right side, it is a credit, and the account is said to be *credited.* The abbreviations for debit and credit are *Dr.* and *Cr.*, respectively.

Whether an increase in a given item is credited or debited depends on the category of the item. By convention, asset and expense increases are recorded as debits, whereas liability, capital, and income increases are recorded as credits. Asset and expenses decreases are recorded as credits, whereas liability, capital, and income decreases are recorded as debits. The following tables summarize the rule.

Assets and Expenses		Liabilities, Capital, and Income	
Dr.	Cr.	Dr.	Cr.
+	−	−	+
(Increases)	(Decreases)	(Decreases)	(Increases)

An account has a debit balance when the sum of its debits exceeds the sum of its credits; it has a credit balance when the sum of the credits is the greater. In *double-entry accounting*, which is in almost universal use, there are equal debit and credit entries for every transaction. Where only two accounts are affected, the debit and credit amounts are equal. If more than two accounts are affected, the total of the debit entries must equal the total of the credit entries.

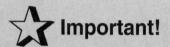

Important!

For every journal entry, debits must equal credits.

The Ledger

The complete set of accounts for a business entry is called a *ledger*. It is the "reference book" of the accounting system and is used to classify and summarize transactions and to prepare data for financial statements. It is also a valuable source of information for managerial purposes, giving, for example, the amount of sales for the period or the cash balance at the end of the period.

The Chart of Accounts

It is desirable to establish a systematic method of identifying and locating each account in the ledger. The *chart of accounts*, sometimes called the *code of accounts*, is a listing of the accounts by title and numerical description. In some companies, the chart of accounts may run to hundreds of items.

   In designing a numbering structure for the accounts, it is important to provide adequate flexibility to permit expansion without having to revise the basic system. Generally, blocks of numbers are assigned to various groups of accounts, such as assets, liabilities, and so on. There are various systems of coding, depending on the needs and desires of the company.

The Trial Balance

As every transaction results in an equal amount of debits and credits in the ledger, the total of all debit entries in the ledger should equal the total of all credit entries. At the end of the accounting period, we check this equality by preparing a two-column schedule called a *trial balance*, which compares the total of all debit balances with the total of all credit balances. The procedure is as follows:

1. List account titles in numerical order.

2. Record balances of each account, entering debit balances in the left column and credit balances in the right column.

3. Add the columns and record the totals.

4. Compare the totals. They must be the same.

If the totals agree, the trial balance is in balance, indicating that debits and credits are equal for the hundreds or thousands of transactions entered in the ledger. While the trial balance provides arithmetic proof of the accuracy of the records, it does not provide theoretical proof. For example, if the purchase of equipment was incorrectly charged to Expense, the trial balance columns may agree, but theoretically the accounts would be wrong, as Expense would be overstated and Equipment understated. In addition to providing proof of arithmetic accuracy in accounts, the trial balance facilitates the preparation of the periodic financial statements. Generally, the trial balance comprises the first two columns of a worksheet, from which financial statements are prepared. The worksheet procedure is discussed in Chapter 8.

Summary

1. To classify and summarize a single item of an account group, we use a form called an _____.

2. The accounts make up a record called a _____.

3. The left side of the account is known as the _____, while the right side of the account is known as the _____.

4. Expenses are debited because they decrease _____.

5. The schedule showing the balance of each account at the end of the period is known as the _____.

Answers: 1. account; 2. ledger; 3. debit, credit; 4. capital; 5. trial balance

Solved Problems

Solved Problem 2.1 Indicate whether the following increases and decreases represent a debit or credit for each particular account.
    (a) Capital is increased
    (b) Cash is decreased
    (c) Accounts Payable is increased
    (d) Rent expense is increased
    (e) Equipment is increased
    (f) Fees income is increased
    (g) Capital is decreased through drawing

Solution:

(a) Cr. (b) Cr. (c) Cr. (d) Dr. (e) Dr. (f) Cr. (g) Dr.

Solved Problem 2.2 Rearrange the following list of accounts and produce a trial balance.

Accounts Payable	$9,000	General expense	1,000
Accounts Receivable	14,000	Notes Payable	11,000
Capital	32,000	Rent expense	5,000
Cash	20,000	Salaries expense	8,000
Drawing	4,000	Supplies	6,000
Equipment	18,000	Supplies expense	2,000
Fees income	26,000		

Solution:

	Dr.	Cr.
Cash	$20,000	
Accounts Receivable	14,000	
Supplies	6,000	
Equipment	18,000	
Accounts Payable		$9,000
Notes Payable		11,000
Capital		32,000
Drawing	4,000	
Fees Income		26,000

Salaries expense	8,000	
Rent expense	5,000	
Supplies expense	2,000	
General expense	1,000	
	$78,000	$78,000

Chapter 3
JOURNALIZING AND POSTING TRANSACTIONS

IN THIS CHAPTER:

- ✔ *Introduction*
- ✔ *The Journal*
- ✔ *Journalizing*
- ✔ *Posting*
- ✔ *Summary*
- ✔ *Solved Problems*

Introduction

In the preceding chapters, we discussed the nature of business transactions and the manner in which they are analyzed and classified. The primary emphasis was the "why" rather than the "how" of accounting operations; we aimed at an understanding of the reason for making the entry in a particular way. We showed the effects of transactions by making entries in T accounts.  However, these entries do not provide the necessary data for a particular transaction, nor do they provide a chronological record of transactions.

The missing information is furnished by the use of an accounting form known as the *journal*.

The Journal

The *journal*, or *day book*, is the book of original entry for accounting data. Afterward, the data is transferred or posted to the ledger, the book of subsequent or secondary entry. The various transactions are evidenced by sales tickets, purchase invoices, check stubs, and so on. On the basis of this evidence, the transactions are entered in chronological order in the journal. The process is called *journalizing*.

A number of different journals may be used in a business. For our purposes, they may be grouped into general journals and specialized journals. The latter type, which are used in businesses with a large number of repetitive transactions, are described in Chapter 6. To illustrate journalizing, we here use the *general journal*, whose standard form is shown below.

General Journal				Page J-1*
Date (1)	Description (2)	P.R. (3)	Debit (4)	Credit (5)
20X3 Oct. 7	Cash	11	$10,000	
	Barbara Ledina, Capital	31		$10,000
	(6) Invested cash in the business			

*Denotes general journal, page 1.

Journalizing

We describe the entries in the general journal according to the numbering in the table above:

1. *Date.* The year, month, and day of the first entry are written in the date column. The year and month do not have to be repeated for the additional entries until a new month occurs or a new page is needed.

2. *Description.* The account title to be debited is entered on the first line, next to the date column. The name of the account to be credited is entered on the line below and indented.

3. *P.R. (Posting Reference).* Nothing is entered in this column until the particular entry is posted, that is, until the amounts are transferred to

the related ledger accounts. The posting process will be described in the next section.

4. *Debit*. The debit amount for each account is entered in this column. Generally, there is only one item, but there could be two or more separate items.

5. *Credit*. The credit amount for each account is entered in this column. Here again, there is generally only one account, but there could be two or more accounts involved with different amounts.

6. *Explanation*. A brief description of the transaction is usually made on the line below the credit. Generally, a blank line is left between the explanation and the next entry.

Posting

The process of transferring information from the journal to the ledger for the purpose of summarizing is called *posting* and is ordinarily carried out in the following steps:

1. *Record the amount and date*. The date and the amounts of the debits and credits are entered in the appropriate accounts.

2. *Record the posting reference in the account*. The number of the journal page is entered in the account

Summary

1. To classify and summarize a single item of an account group, we use a form called an _____.

2. The accounts make up a record called a _____.

3. The left side of the account is known as the _____, while the right side of the account is known as the _____.

4. Expenses are debited because they decrease _____.

5. The schedule showing the balance of each account at the end of the period is known as the _____.

Answers: 1. account; 2. ledger; 3. debit, credit; 4. capital; 5. trial balance

Solved Problems

Solved Problem 3.1 Below each entry, write a brief explanation of the transaction that might appear in the general journal.

(a) Equipment	10,000	
Cash		2,000
Accounts Payable		8,000
(b) Accounts Payable	8,000	
Notes Payable		8,000
(c) Notes Payable	8,000	
Cash		8,000

Solution:

(a) purchase of equipment, 20% for cash, balance on account
(b) notes payable in settlement of accounts payable
(c) settlement of notes payable

Solved Problem 3.2 Dr. Patrick Wallace began his practice, investing in the business the following assets:

Cash	$12,000
Supplies	1,400
Equipment	22,600
Furniture	10,000

Record the opening entry in the journal.

Solution:

Cash	12,000	
Supplies	1,400	
Equipment	22,600	
Furniture	10,000	
P. Wallace, Capital		46,000

Solved Problem 3.3 If, in Solved Problem 3.2, Dr. Wallace owed a balance of $3,500 on the equipment, what would the opening entry be?

Solution:

Cash	12,000		
Supplies	1,400		
Equipment	22,600		
Furniture	10,000		
	Accounts Payable	3,500	
	P. Wallace, Capital	42,500	

Chapter 4
FINANCIAL STATEMENTS

IN THIS CHAPTER:

✔ *Introduction*
✔ *Income Statement*
✔ *Accrual Basis and Cash Basis of Accounting*
✔ *Balance Sheet*
✔ *Capital Statement*
✔ *Classified Financial Statements*
✔ *Summary*
✔ *Solved Problems*

Introduction

The two principal questions that the owner of a business asks periodically are:

1. What is my net income (profit)?
2. What is my capital?

The simple balance of assets against liabilities and capital provided by the accounting equation is insufficient to give complete answers. For the first, we must know the type and amount of income and the type and

17

amount of each expense for the period in question. For second, it is necessary to obtain the type and amount of each asset, liability, and capital account at the end of the period. The information to answer the first question is provided by the income statement, and information to answer the second comes from the balance sheet.

⭐ **Note!**

Each heading of a financial statement answers the questions "who," "what," and "when."

Income Statement

The *income statement* may be defined as *a summary of the revenue (income), expenses, and net income of a business entity for a specific period of time.* This may also be called a profit and loss statement, an operating statement, or a statement of operations. Let us review the meanings of the elements entering into the income statement.

Revenue. The increase in capital resulting from the delivery of goods or rendering of services by the business. In amount, the revenue is equal to the cash and receivables gained in compensation for the goods delivered or services rendered.

Expenses. The decrease in capital caused by the business's revenue-producing operations. In amount, the expense is equal to the value of goods and services used up or consumed in obtaining revenue.

Net income. The increase in capital resulting from profitable operation of a business; it is the excess of revenue over expenses for the accounting period.

It is important to note that a *cash receipt* qualifies as revenue only if it serves to increase capital. Similarly, a *cash payment* is an expense only if it decreases capital. Thus, for instance, borrowing cash from a bank does not contribute to revenue.

In many companies, there are hundreds and perhaps thousands of income and expense transactions in a month. To lump all these transactions under one account would be very cumbersome and would, in addition, make it impossible to show relationships among the various items. To solve this problem, we set up a temporary set of income and expense accounts. The net difference of these accounts, the net profit or net loss, is then transferred as one figure to the capital account.

Don't Forget!

The income statement is also known as a profit and loss statement, an operating statement, or a statement of operations.

Accrual Basis and Cash Basis of Accounting

Because an income statement pertains to a definite period of time, it becomes necessary to determine just when an item of revenue or expense is to be accounted for. Under the *accrual basis* of accounting, revenue is recognized only when it is earned and expense is recognized only when it is incurred. This differs significantly from the *cash basis* of accounting, which recognizes revenue and expense generally with the receipt and payment of cash. Essential to the accrual basis is the matching of expenses with the revenue that they helped produce. Under the accrual system, the accounts are adjusted at the end of the accounting period to properly reflect the revenue earned and the cost and expenses applicable to the period.

Most business firms use the accrual basis, whereas individuals and professional people generally use the cash basis. Ordinarily, the cash basis is not suitable when there are significant amounts of inventories, receivables, and payables.

Balance Sheet

The information needed for the balance sheet items are the net balances at the end of the period, rather than the total for the period as in the income statement. Thus, management wants to know the balance of cash in the bank and the balance of inventory, equipment, etc., on hand at the end of the period.

The *balance sheet* may then be defined as a *statement showing the assets, liabilities, and capital of a business entity at a specific date.* This statement is also called a statement of financial position or statement of financial condition.

In preparing a balance sheet, it is not necessary to make any further analysis of the data. The needed data, that is, the balance of the asset, liability, and capital accounts, are already available.

The close relationship of the income statement and the balance sheet is apparent. The income statement is the connecting link between two balance sheets, the previous year and the current year.

You Need to Know

The income and expense items are actually a further analysis of the capital account.

Capital Statement

Instead of showing the details of the capital account in the balance sheet, we may show the changes in a separate form called the *capital statement.* This is the more common treatment. The capital statement begins with the balance of the capital account on the first day of the period, adds increases in capital (example: net income) and subtracts decreases in capital (example: withdrawals) to reach the balance of the capital account at the end of the period.

Classified Financial Statements

Financial statements become more useful when the individual items are classified into significant groups for comparison and financial analysis. The classifications relating to the balance sheet will be discussed in this section, while the classification of the income statement will be shown in a later chapter.

The Balance Sheet

The balance sheet becomes a more useful statement for comparison and financial analysis if the asset and liability groups are classified. For example, an important index of the financial state of a business, derivable from the classified balance sheet, is the ratio of current assets to current liabilities. This current ratio should generally be at least 2:1; that is, current assets should be twice current liabilities. For our purposes, we will designate the following classifications.

Assets	Liabilities
Current	Current
Property, plant and equipment	Long-Term
Other Assets	

Current Assets. Assets reasonably expected to be converted into cash or used in the current operation of the business (generally taken as one year). Examples are cash, notes receivable, accounts receivable, inventory, and prepaid expenses.

Property, plant and equipment. Long-lived assets used in the production of goods or services. These assets, sometimes called *fixed assets* or *plant assets*, are used in the operation of the business rather than being held for sale, as are inventory items.

Other Assets. Various assets other than current assets, fixed assets, or assets to which specific captions are given. For instance, the caption "Investments" would be used if significant sums were invested. Often companies show a caption for intangible assets such as patents or goodwill. In other cases, there may be a separate caption for deferred charges. If, however, the amounts are not large in relation to total assets, the various items may be grouped under one caption, "Other Assets."

Current Liabilities. Debts that must be satisfied from current assets within the next operating period, usually one year. Examples are accounts payable, notes payable, the current portion of long-term debt, and various accrued items such as salaries payable and taxes payable.

Long-term liabilities. Liabilities that are payable beyond the next year. The most common examples are bonds payable and mortgages payable.

 **Note!**

Most businesses operate using the accrual method of accounting. Under the accrual basis of accounting, revenue is recognized only when it is earned and expense is recognized only when it is incurred.

Summary

1. Another term for an accounting period is an _____.
2. The statement that shows net income for the period is known as the _____ statement.
3. Two groups of items that make up the income statement are _____ and _____.
4. Assets must equal _____.
5. Expense and income must be matched in the same _____.

Answers: 1. accounting statement; 2. income; 3. income, expense; 4. liabilities and capital; 5. year or period

Solved Problems

Solved Problem 4.1 Indicate the name of the account group—Income (I), Expense (E), Asset (A), Liability (L), or Capital (C)—in which each of the following accounts belong.

(a) Accounts payable

(b) Accounts receivable

(c) Building

(d) Supplies

(e) Cash

(f) Drawing

(g) Equipment

(h) Fees income

(i) Interest expense

(j) Interest income

(k) Notes payable

(l) Rent income

Solution:

(a) L (b) A (c) A (d) A (e) A (f) C (g) A (h) I (i) E (j) I (k) L (l) I

Solved Problem 4.2 Below is an income statement with some of the information missing. Fill in the information needed to complete the income statement.

Sales Income   (b)

    Operating Expenses:

    Wages Expense $16,910

    Rent Expense   (a)

    Utilities Expense   3,150

    Total Expenses   32,150

    Net Income $41,300

Solution:

(a) 12,090 (b) $73,450

Chapter 5

ADJUSTING AND CLOSING PROCEDURES

IN THIS CHAPTER:

Introduction: The Accrual Basis of Accounting

Accounting records are kept on the *accrual* basis, except in the case of very small businesses. *To accrue* means *to collect or accumulate*. This means that revenue is recognized when earned, regardless of when cash is actually collected and expense is matched to the revenue, regardless of when cash is paid out. Most revenue is earned when goods or services are delivered. At this time, title to the goods or services is transferred and a legal obligation to pay for such goods or services is created. Some revenue, such as rental income, is recognized on a time basis, and is earned when  the specified period of time has passed. The accrual concept demands that expenses be kept in step with revenue, so that each month sees only that month's expenses applied against the revenue for that month. The necessary matching is brought about through a type of journal entry. In this chapter, we shall discuss these adjusting entries, and also the closing entries through which the adjusted balances are ultimately transferred to balance sheet accounts at the end of the fiscal year.

Adjusting Entries Covering Recorded Data

To adjust expense or income items that have already been recorded, a reclassification is required; that is, amounts have to be transferred from an asset, one of the prepaid expenses accounts (e.g., Prepaid Insurance), to an expense account (Insurance Expense). The following five examples will show how adjusting entries are made for the principal types of recorded expenses.

Prepaid Insurance
Assume that on April 1, a business paid a $1,200 premium for one year's insurance in advance. This represents an increase in one asset (prepaid expense) and a decrease in another asset (cash). Thus the entry would be:

Prepaid Insurance	1,200	
Cash		1,200

At the end of April, one-twelfth of the $1,200, or $100, has expired. Therefore, an adjustment has to be made, decreasing or crediting Prepaid Insurance and increasing or debiting Insurance Expense. The entry would be:

```
Insurance Expense          100
     Prepaid Insurance              100
```

Thus, $100 would be shown as Insurance Expense in the income statement for April and the balance of $1,100 would be shown as part of Prepaid Insurance in the balance sheet.

Prepaid Rent

Assume that on April 1 a business paid $1,800 to cover the rent for the next three months. The full amount would have been recorded as a prepaid expense in April. Since there is a three-month period involved, the rent expense each month is $600. The balance of Prepaid Rent would be $1,200 at the beginning of May. The adjusting entry for April would be:

```
Rent Expense          600
     Prepaid Rent              600
```

Supplies

A type of prepayment that is somewhat different from those previously described is the payment for office supplies or factory supplies. Assume that on April 1, $400 worth of supplies were purchased. There were none on hand before. This would increase the asset Supplies and decrease the asset Cash. At the end of April, when expense and revenue were to be matched and statements prepared, a count of the supplies on hand will be made. Assume that the inventory count shows that $250 of supplies are still on hand. Then the amount consumed during April was $150. The two entries are as follows:

```
Apr. 1   Supplies              400
             Cash                     400
     30   Supplies Expense     150
             Supplies                 150
```

Supplies Expense of $150 will be included in the April income statement; Supplies of $250 will be included as an asset on the balance sheet of April 30.

Accumulated Depreciation

In the previous three adjusting entries, the balances of the assets mentioned were all reduced. These assets usually lose their value in a relatively short period of time. However, assets that have a longer life expectancy (such as a building) are treated differently because the accounting profession wants to keep a balance sheet record of the equipment's original, or historical, cost. Thus the adjusting entry needed to reflect the true value of the long-term asset each year must allocate its original cost, known as depreciation. In order to accomplish the objectives of keeping original cost of the equipment and also maintaining a running total of the depreciation allocated, we must create a new account entitled Accumulated Depreciation. This account, known as a contra asset (an asset that has the opposite balance to its asset), summarizes and accumulates the amount of depreciation over the equipment's total useful life. Assume that machinery costing $15,000 was purchased on February 1 of the current year and was expected to last ten years. With the straight-line method of depreciation (equal charges each period), the depreciation would be $1,500 a year, or $125 a month. The adjusting entry would be as follows:

Depreciation Expense	125	
Accumulated Depreciation		125

At the end of April, Accumulated Depreciation would have a balance of $375, representing three months' accumulated depreciation. The account would be shown in the balance sheet as follows:

Machinery	$15,000	
Less: Accumulated Depreciation	375	$14,625

Adjusting Entries Covering Unrecorded Data

In the previous section we discussed various kinds of adjustments to accounts to which entries had already been made. Now we consider those instances in which an expense has been incurred or an income earned but the applicable amount has not been recorded during the month. For example, if salaries are paid on a weekly basis, the last week of the month may run into the next month. If April ends on a Tuesday, then the first two days of the week will apply to April and will be an April expense, whereas the last three days will be a May expense. To arrive at the proper total for salaries for the month of April, we must include, along with the April payrolls that were paid in April, the two days' salary that was not paid until May. Thus, we make an entry to accrue the two days' salary.

Accrued Salaries

Assume that April 30 falls on Tuesday. Then, two days of that week will apply to April and three days to May. The payroll is $500 per day, $2,500 per week. For this example, $1,000 would thus apply to April and $1,500 to May. The entry would be as follows:

April 30 Salaries Expense	1,000	
Salaries Payable		1,000

When the payment of the payroll is made—on May 8—the entry would be as follows:

May 8 Salaries Expense	1,500	
Salaries Payable	1,000	
Cash		2,500

As can be seen above, $1,000 was charged to expense in April and $1,500 in May. The debit to Accrued Salaries Payable of $1,000 in May merely canceled the credit entry made in April, when the liability was set up for the April salaries expense

Closing Entries

After the income statement and balance sheet have been prepared, a summary account—known as Income Summary—is set up. Then, by means of closing entries, each expense account is credited so as to produce a zero balance, and the total amount for the closed-out accounts is debited to Income Summary. Similarly, the individual revenue accounts are closed out by debiting them and their total amount is credited to the summary account. Thus, the new fiscal year starts with zero balances in the income and expense accounts, whereas the Income Summary balance gives the net income or the net loss for the old year.

Note!

In order to transfer balances from an asset account to an expense account, an adjusting entry is required. Adjusting entries are used throughout the year to transfer these prepaid amounts to expense accounts as the asset is used.

T. Drew
Trial Balance
January 31, 20X3

Cash	$3,900	
Supplies	100	
Furniture	2,000	
Accounts Payable		$ 800
T. Drew, Capital		4,000
T. Drew, Drawing	400	
Fees Income		2,500
Rent Expense	500	
Salaries Expense	200	
Supplies Expense	200	
	$7,300	$7,300

The closing entries are as follows:

Close out revenue accounts. Debit the individual income accounts and credit their total to Income Summary.

Jan. 31 Fees Income   2,500
                Income Summary   2,500

Close out expense accounts. Credit the individual expense accounts and debit their total to Income Summary.

Jan. 31 Income Summary   900
                Rent Expense   500
                Salaries Expense   200
                Supplies Expense   200

Close out the Income Summary account. If there is a profit, the credit made for total income in the first entry above will exceed the debit made for total expense in the second entry above. Therefore to close out the balance to zero, a debit entry will be made to Income Summary. A credit will be made to the capital account to transfer the net income for the period. If expenses exceed income, then a loss has been sustained and a credit will be made to Income Summary and a debit to the capital account. Based on the information given, the entry is:

>Jan. 31 Income Summary 1,600
>Capital Account 1,600

Close out the drawing account. The drawing account is credited for the total amount of the drawings for the period, and the capital account is debited for that amount. The difference between net income and drawing for the period represents the net change in the capital account for the period. The net income of $1,600 less drawings of $400 results in a net increase of $1,200 in the capital account. The closing entry is as follows:

>Jan. 31 Capital Account 300
>Drawing Account 300

Ruling Accounts

After the posting of the closing entries, all revenue and expense accounts and the summary accounts are closed. When ruling an account where only one debit and one credit exist, a double rule is drawn below the entry across the debit and credit money columns. The date and reference columns also have a double rule, in order to separate the transactions from the period just ended and the entry to be made in the subsequent period.

Post-Closing Trial Balance

After the closing entries have been made and the accounts ruled, only balance sheet accounts—assets, liabilities, and capital—remain open. It is desirable to produce another trial balance to ensure that the accounts are in balance. This is known as a *post-closing trial balance*.

Summary

1. The basis of accounting that recognizes revenue when it is earned, regardless of when cash is received, and matches the expenses to the revenue, regardless of when cash is paid out, is known as the _____.

2. An adjusting entry that records the expired amount of prepaid insurance would create the _____ account.

3. The revenue and expense accounts are closed out to the summary account known as _____.

4. Eventually, all income, expense, and drawing accounts, including summaries, are closed into the _____ account.

5. The post-closing trial balance involves only _____, _____, and _____ accounts.

Answers: 1. accrual basis; 2. insurance expense; 3. income summary; 4. capital; 5. asset, liability, capital

Solved Problems

Solved Problem 5.1 A business pays weekly salaries of $10,000 on Friday for the five-day work week. Show the adjusting entry when the fiscal period ends on (a) Tuesday; (b) Thursday.

Solution:

(a)	Salaries Expense	4,000	
	Salaries Payable		4,000
(b)	Salaries Expense	8,000	
	Salaries Payable		8,000

Solved Problem 5.2 An insurance policy covering a two-year period was purchased on November 1 for $600. The amount was debited to Prepaid Insurance. Show the adjusting entry for the two-month period ending December 31.

Solution:

Insurance Expense	50*	
Prepaid Insurance		50

* ($600/ 2 years) multiplied by (2/12) years equals $50

Solved Problem 5.3 Machinery costing $12,000, purchased November 30, is being depreciated at the rate of 10 percent per year. Show the adjusting entry for December 31.

Solution:

Depreciation Expense—Machinery	100*	
Accumulated Depreciation—Machinery		100

*$12,000 times 10% per year times (1/12) year equals $100

Solved Problem 5.4

   (a) The balance in the Prepaid Insurance account, before adjustments, is $1,800, and the amount expired during the year is $1,200. The amount needed for the adjusting entry required is _____.

   (b) A business pays weekly salaries of $4,000 on Friday. The amount of the adjusting entry necessary at the end of the fiscal period ending on Wednesday is _____.

   (c) On December 31, the end of the fiscal year, the supplies account had a balance before adjustment of $650. The fiscal supply inventory account on December 31 is $170. The amount of the adjusting entry is

_____.

Solution:
(a) $1,200
(b) $2,400
(c) $480

Chapter 6

REPETITIVE TRANSACTIONS– THE SALES AND THE PURCHASES JOURNALS

IN THIS CHAPTER:

- ✔ Introduction
- ✔ Special Ledgers
- ✔ Sales Returns and Discounts
- ✔ Types of Ledger Account Forms
- ✔ Purchases As a Cost
- ✔ Trade Discounts
- ✔ Purchase Control
- ✔ Purchase Invoices
- ✔ Purchases Journal
- ✔ Subsidiary Accounts Payable Ledger

✔ *Return of Merchandise*
✔ *Purchase Discounts*
✔ *Summary*
✔ *Solved Problems*

Introduction

In the previous chapters, each transaction was recorded by
first placing an entry in the general journal and then posting
the entry to the related accounts in the general ledger. This
system, however, is both time-consuming and wasteful. It is
much simpler and more efficient to group together those
transactions that are repetitive, such as sales, purchases,
cash receipts, and cash payments, and place each of them in
a special journal.

Many types of transactions may require the use of special journals,
for example, receipt or payment of cash and purchase or sale of goods or
services.

The number and design of the special journals will vary, depending
on the needs of a particular business. The special journals used in a typical firm are as follows:

Name of Special Journal	Abbreviation	Type of Transaction
Cash receipts journal	CR	All cash received
Cash disbursements journal	CD	All cash paid out
Purchases journal	P	All purchases on account
Sales journal	S	All sales on account

In addition to these four special journals, a general journal (J) is used
for recording transactions that do not fit into any of the four types above.
The general journal is also used for the recording of adjusting and closing entries at the end of the accounting period.

Note!

Only sales on account are recorded in the sales journal; cash sales are recorded in the receipts journal.

Special Ledgers

Further simplification of the general ledger is brought about by the use of subsidiary ledgers. In particular, for those businesses that sell goods on credit and that find it necessary to maintain a separate account for each customer and each creditor, the use of a special accounts receivable ledger eliminates the need to make multiple entries in the general ledger.

The advantages of special or subsidiary ledgers are similar to the advantages of special journals. These are:

1. Reduces ledger detail. Most of the information will be in the subsidiary ledger, and the general ledger will be reserved chiefly for summary or total figures. Therefore, it will be easier to prepare the financial statements.

2. Permits better division of labor. Here again, each special or subsidiary ledger may be handled by a different person. Therefore, one person may work on the general ledger accounts while another person may work simultaneously on the subsidiary ledger.

3. Permits a different sequence of accounts. In the general ledger, it is desirable to have the accounts in the same sequence as in the balance sheet and income statement. As a further aid, it is desirable to use numbers to locate and reference the accounts. However, in connection with accounts receivable, which involves names of customers or companies, it is preferable to have the accounts in alphabetical sequence.

4. Permits better internal control. Better control is maintained if a person other than the person responsible for the general ledger is responsible for the subsidiary ledger. The general ledger accounts as a controlling account, and the subsidiary ledger must agree with the control. No unauthorized entry could be made in the subsidiary ledger, as it would immediately put that record out of balance with the control account.

The idea of *control accounts*, introduced above, is an important one in accounting. Any group of similar accounts may be removed from the general ledger and a controlling account substituted for it. Not only is another level of error protection thereby provided, but the time need to prepare the general ledger trial balance and the financial statements becomes further reduced.

In order to be capable of supplying information concerning the business's accounts receivable, a firm needs a separate account for each customer. These customer accounts are grouped together in a subsidiary ledger known as the *accounts receivable ledger.* Each time the accounts receivable ledger must also be increased or decreased by the same amount. The customers' accounts are usually kept in alphabetical order and include, besides outstanding balances, information such as address, phone number, credit terms, and other pertinent items.

Remember

The advantages of subsidiary ledgers are:
- reduces ledger detail
- permits better division of labor
- permits a different sequence of accounts
- permits better internal control.

Sales Returns and Discounts

If, during the year, many transactions occur in which customers return goods bought on account, a special journal known as the *sales returns journal* would be used. However, where sales returns are infrequent, the general journal is sufficient.

The entry to record return of sales on account in the general journal would be:

Sales Returns	800	
Accounts Receivable		800

The accounts receivable account, which is credited, is posted both in the accounts receivable controlling account and in the accounts receivable ledger. If the Sales Returns involve payment of cash, it would appear in the cash disbursements journal. Sales Returns appear in the income statement as a reduction of Sales Income.

To induce a buyer to make payment before the amount is due, the seller may allow the buyer to deduct a certain percentage of the bill. If payment is due within a stated number of days after the date of invoice, the number of days will usually be preceded by the letter "n," signifying net. For example, bills due in 30 days would be indicated by n/30.

You Need to Know

A 2 percent discount offered if payment is made within 10 days would be indicated by 2/10. If the buyer has a choice of either paying the amount less 2 percent within the 10-day period or paying the entire bill within 30 days, the terms would be written as 2/10, n/30.

Types of Ledger Account Forms

The T account has been used for most illustrations of accounts thus far. The disadvantage of the T account is that it requires totaling the debit and the credit columns in order to find the balance. As it is necessary to have the balance of a customer's or creditor's account available at any given moment, an alternative form of the ledger, the *three-column account*, may be used. The advantage of this form is that an extra column, "Balance," is provided, so that the amount the customer owes, or the creditor is owed, is always shown. As each transaction is recorded, the balance is updated. Below is an illustration of an accounts receivable ledger account using this form.

Accounts Receivable, M. Gersten

Date	Debit	Credit	Balance
Jan. 2	650		650
4	409		1,059
8		500	559

Purchases As a Cost

Before any firm can sell merchandise, it must purchase goods to be resold. Purchasing goods for resale is synonymous with incurring an expense. Cost accounts are similar to expense accounts, because both decrease the owners' capital and both are temporary. In order to record the cost of all goods bought during an accounting period, a new account, Purchases, must be established.

 **Note!**

Expenses are necessary in order to operate a business, but costs are incurred in order to acquire goods for resale.

Trade Discounts

Manufacturers and wholesalers publish catalogs in order to describe their products and list their retail prices. Usually, they offer deductions from these list prices to dealers who buy in large quantities. These deductions are known as *trade discounts*. By offering these discounts, a business can *adjust* a price at which it is willing to bill its goods without changing the list price in the catalog.

Purchase Control

Some procedures for proper merchandising control affect the purchase of items for resale:

1. When items are needed for resale, a *purchase requisition* is made and sent to the purchasing department.

2. The purchasing department prepares a *purchase order*, after checking all conditions of the purchase. This order consists of the price, quantity, and description of goods to be ordered. It may also show information regarding payment terms and costs of transportation (freight).

3. When the goods are received, a *purchase invoice* is enclosed, showing the amount of the goods shipped and their related costs. This document provides the basis for recording the purchase.

4. Before paying the invoice, the accounts payable department should verify the contents of the shipment of goods received and the correctness of the purchase order to ensure that what was ordered was received.

Purchase Invoices

In most businesses, purchases are made regularly and are evidenced by purchase invoices to creditors. A purchase invoice is the source document that supplies the information for recording goods on account. Such information would include:

1. Seller's name and address
2. Date of purchase and invoice number
3. Method of shipment
4. Terms of the purchase transaction
5. Type and quantity of goods shipped
6. Cost of goods billed

Where there are many transactions for purchases of merchandise for resale, for supplies or equipment, the labor-saving features of a special purchases journal should be utilized.

Purchases Journal

The basic principles that apply to the sales journal also apply to the purchases journal. However, a single-column purchases journal is too limited to be practicable, as businesses do not usually restrict their credit purchases only to merchandise bought for resale. Various kinds of goods (office and store supplies, equipment) are bought on a charge basis. Therefore, the purchases journal can be expanded with special columns to record those accounts that are frequently affected by credit purchase transactions.

Subsidiary Accounts Payable Ledger

Early in this chapter, a new subsidiary ledger, called Accounts Receivable, was created for all a company's customers. A firm that purchases on account would do the same thing, because the credit balance in Accounts Payable represents the total amount owed by the company for purchases on account.

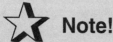 **Note!**

Because the account shows only the total liability to all sellers, the need for a subsidiary record for each creditor in a separate ledger is apparent.

Posting to the Subsidiary Ledger

During the month, each individual credit entry is posted from the purchases journal to the creditor's account in the subsidiary ledger. A check mark is placed in the posting reference column in the purchases journal to show that the amount has been posted. The check mark is used because the individual creditor's accounts are not numbered.

    1. When a purchase on account is made, the invoice becomes the basis for the credit to the creditor's ledger account.

    2. When a payment is made, the account is debited.

    3. Any credit balance in a subsidiary account represents an unpaid balance owed to that particular firm.

    No postings are made to the general ledger until the end of the month, when all the amounts are accumulated into one total. It is at this time that the total amount of all purchases for the month, as well as other debits, including supplies, equipment, land, and so on, are posted to the respective accounts and then credited to the accounts payable controlling account in the general ledger.

The total of all the credit amounts posted to the accounts payable ledger must equal the total credit to the controlling account in the general ledger. When the postings from the purchases journal are completed for the month, the ledgers should balance.

In order to prove that the subsidiary ledger is in agreement with the controlling account of the general ledger, a schedule of accounts payable is prepared. This schedule is the total of all the balances of each of the credit accounts. Their total must equal that of the controlling accounts payable.

Return of Merchandise

At times, a business ordering goods might find that purchases were received damaged or not meeting certain specifications. Regardless of the reason, these goods would be returned to the seller and are known as *returns*. An *allowance* would be granted by which the seller gives the purchaser either a refund or a credit adjustment. Instead of crediting the account Purchases for the return, correct accounting procedures would set up a new account, *Purchases Returns and Allowances*. This contra account provides a separate record of the cost reduction and allows management to exercise better control of its merchandise purchases. Since Purchases Returns and Allowances is a contra account, its normal balance will be a credit.

You Need to Know

The balance of the Purchases Returns and Allowances account appears on the income statement as a reduction of Purchases. The difference is called Net Purchases.

Purchase Discounts

To induce a buyer to make payment before the amount is due, the seller may allow the buyer to deduct a certain percentage from the total. If payment is due within a stated number of days after the date of invoice, the number of days will usually be preceded by the letter "n," signifying net. For example, bills due in 30 days would be indicated by n/30. A 2 percent discount offered if payment is made within 10 days would be indicated by 2/10. If the buyer has a choice of either paying the amount less 2 percent within the 10-day period or paying the entire bill within 30 days, the terms would be written as 2/10, n/30.

If the buyer chooses to pay within the discount period, a new contra account, *Purchase Discount*, would be created and would appear as a reduction of Purchases in the cost of goods sold section of the income statement.

Summary

1. When transactions that are repetitive in nature are grouped together, they are placed in a _____ journal.

2. All sales _____ are recorded in the sales journal.

3. The _____ ledger is used to maintain a separate account for each customer.

4. Deductions from list or retail price offered by manufacturers or wholesalers are known as _____.

5. Postings to the general ledger are made _____, whereas subsidiary accounts are posted _____.

Answers: 1. special; 2. on account; 3. accounts receivable; 4. trade discounts; 5. at the end of the month, immediately

Solved Problems

Solved Problem 6.1 For each of the following transactions, indicate in which journal—Sales Journal (S), General Journal (G), or Cash Journal (C)—it should be recorded:
   (a) Sale of merchandise to Marsha Byman on account, $400
   (b) Sale of merchandise to Jim Dosen for cash, $150
   (c) Cash refunded to Jim Dosen for goods returned
   (d) Marsha Byman returned part of the goods sold for credit, $100

Solution:
(a) S (b) C (c) C (d) G

Solved Problem 6.2 Which of the transactions in Solved Problem 6.1 should be posted to the subsidiary ledger?

Solution:
Transactions (a) and (d), because sales were on account. Transactions (b) and (c) involved cash, thus creating no accounts receivable.

Solved Problem 6.3 Cambruzzi Company was established in December of the current year. Its sales of merchandise on account and related returns and allowances during the remainder of the month are described below.

Dec. 15 Sold merchandise on account to A Co., $850
    19 Sold merchandise on account to B Co., $800
    20 Sold merchandise on account to C Co., $1,200
    22 Issued Credit memo for $40 to B Co. for merchandise return
    24 Sold merchandise on account to B Co., $1,650
    25 Sold additional merchandise on account to B. Co, $900
    26 Issued Credit memo for $25 to A Co. for merchandise return
    27 Sold additional merchandise on account to C Co., $1,600

Record the transactions for December in the sales journal and/or general journal.

Solution:

Sales Journal

Date	Account Debited	Amount
12/15	A Co.	850
12/19	B Co.	800
12/20	C Co.	1,200
12/24	D Co.	1,650
12/25	B Co.	900
12/27	C Co.	1,600
		7,000

General Journal

Date	Description	Dr.	Cr.
12/22	Sales Returns	40	
	Accounts Receivable		40
12/26	Sales Returns	25	
	Accounts Receivable		25

IN THIS CHAPTER:

✔ *Introduction*
✔ *Cash Receipts Journal*
✔ *Cash Disbursements Journal*
✔ *Combination Cash Journal*
✔ *Summary*
✔ *Solved Problems*

Introduction

We have observed that the use of the sales journal and the purchases journal enables us to carry out the journalizing and posting processes more efficiently. These special journals save space by permitting the recording of an entry on one line and the posting of total columns rather than individual figures. This is also true of the cash receipts journal and the cash disbursements journal.

Cash Receipts Journal

All receipts (cash and checks) received by a business are recorded daily in either a *cash receipts* or a *combination cash journal*. For control purposes, the cash handling and recording processes are separated. In addition, whenever feasible, receipts are deposited intact (without cash disbursements being made from them) daily. The most common sources of cash receipts are cash sales and collections on account.

The steps for recording and posting the cash receipts journal are described below:

1. Record the cash receipts in the cash receipts journal, *debiting* Cash for the amount received and *crediting* the appropriate column. Indicate in the Account Credited space:

(a) The customer's name (subsidiary account) for collections on account.

(b) An explanation (cash sale) for cash sales.

(c) The title of the item involved in the Sundry account.

2. After recording collections on account, post *by date* to the appropriate subsidiary ledger account:

(a) In the customer's account, record the amount *credited* and indicate the source of the entry in the Posting Reference column.

(b) Put a checkmark in the Posting Reference column of the journal to indicate that a posting has been completed.

3. At the *end* of the month, total all columns of the journal and check to be sure that all the columns balance before posting. If they do balance, put a double line under the column totals.

4. Post the column totals to the appropriate general ledger account:

(a) In the appropriate general ledger account, record the amount *debited* or *credited* and indicate the source of the entry in the Posting Reference column.

(b) Place the account number of the account posted to *under* the column totals, to indicate that a posting has been completed.

(c) Each item in the Sundry account is posted individually to the general ledger. The total of the Sundry account is not posted.

 Important Point!

For control purposes, the cash handling and recording processes are separated. In addition, whenever feasible, receipts are deposited intact daily.

Cash Disbursements Journal

The cash disbursements journal is used to record all transactions that reduce cash. These transactions may arise from payments to creditors, from cash purchases, and from the payment of expenses, as well as personal withdrawals.

The procedure for recording and posting the cash disbursements journal parallels that of the cash receipts journal:

1. A check is written each time a payment is made; the check numbers provide a convenient reference, and they help in controlling cash and in reconciling the bank account.

2. The cash credit column is posted in total to the general ledger at the end of the month.

3. Debits to Accounts Payable represent cash paid to creditors. These individual amounts will be posted to the creditors' accounts in the accounts payable subsidiary ledger. At the end of the month, the total of the accounts payable column is posted to the general ledger.

4. The Sundry column is used to record debits for any account that cannot be entered in the other special columns. These would include purchases of equipment, inventory, payment of expenses, and cash withdrawals. Each item is posted separately to the general ledger. The total of the Sundry column is not posted.

Combination Cash Journal

Some companies, primarily for convenience, prefer to record all cash transactions (receipts and disbursements) in one journal. This combination cash journal uses basically the same account columns as the cash receipts and cash disbursements journals, but with a different arrangement of accounts.

This journal makes it easier to keep track on a day-to-day basis of changes in the Cash account, since the debit and credit to Cash are adjacent to one another.

Summary

1. For cash control purposes, cash handling and _____ must be separated.

2. The cash column in the cash receipts journal is _____, whereas the same column in the cash payments journal is _____ whenever cash is received or disbursed.

3. The _____ journal is used to record all transactions that reduce cash.

4. _____ to Accounts Payable represent cash paid to creditors.

5. The _____ journal contains all records of cash transactions (receipts and disbursements).

Answers: 1. recording; 2. debited, credited; 3. cash disbursements; 4. debits; 5. combination cash

Solved Problems

Solved Problem 7.1 A sales invoice totaling $3,000 and dated January 14 has discount terms of 2/10, n/30. If it is paid January 23, what would be the entry to record this transaction?

Solution:

Cash	2,940	
Sales Discount	60	
Accounts Receivable		3,000

Solved Problem 7.2 Record the following transactions in the cash receipts journal:

3/2	Received $600 from J. Kappala in settlement of her account
3/10	Received $615 from B. Elder in settlement of his account
3/14	Cash sales for a 2-week period, $4,400
3/28	Sold $200 of office supplies to Smith Company (not a merchandise item)
3/30	Owner made additional investment, $1,500
3/30	Cash sales for the last two weeks, $2,600

Solution:

				Cash Receipts Journal		CR-1
Date	Account Credited	P.R.	Cash Dr.	Acct. Rec. Cr.	Sales Income Cr.	Sundry Cr.
Mar 2	J. Kappala	✓	600	600		
10	B. Elder	✓	615	615		
14	Cash Sales	✓	4,400		4,400	
28	Office Supplies	15	200			200
30	Capital	31	1,500			1,500
30	Cash Sales	✓	2,600		2,600	
			9,915	1,215	7,000	1,700

Chapter 8
SUMMARIZING AND REPORTING VIA THE WORKSHEET

IN THIS CHAPTER:

- ✔ *Introduction*
- ✔ *Worksheet Procedures for a Service Business*
- ✔ *Summary*
- ✔ *Solved Problems*

Introduction

The recording of transactions and the adjusting and closing procedures have been discussed in previous chapters. It is reasonable to expect that among the hundreds of computations and clerical tasks involved some errors will occur, such as posting a debit as a credit. Today many financial records are maintained on the computer or on mechanical bookkeeping systems. The use of machine time to correct errors can be very costly and may provoke questions from financial managers.

49

One of the best ways yet developed of avoiding errors in the permanent accounting records, and also of simplifying the work at the end of the period, is to make use of an informal record called a *worksheet*.

Worksheet Procedures for a Service Business

We are already familiar with the types of accounts found in a service business—that is, a business in which revenue comes from services rendered —so we shall first discuss the worksheet for such a business.

The work sheet is usually prepared in pencil on a large sheet of accounting stationery called *analysis paper*. On the worksheet, the ledger accounts are adjusted, balanced, and arranged in proper form for preparing the financial statements. All procedures can be reviewed quickly, and the adjusting and closing entries can be made in the formal records with less chance of error.

 **Note!**

With the data for the income statement and balance sheet already proved out on the worksheet, these statements can be prepared more quickly.

For a typical service business, we may suppose the worksheet to have eight monetary columns; namely, a debit and credit column for four groups of figures: trial balance, adjustments, income statement, and balance sheet.

A ten-column work sheet also is used, consisting of:
1. Trial balance
2. Adjustments
3. Adjusted trial balance
4. Income statement, and
5. Balance sheet.

The adjusted trial balance columns simplify the extension to the financial statement columns. The steps for completing the worksheet are:

1. Enter the trial balance figures from the ledger.

2. Enter the adjustments.

3. Extend the adjusted trial balance and the adjustment figures to either the income statement or balance sheet columns.

4. Total the income statement columns and the balance sheet columns.

5. Enter the net income or net loss.

Use the following procedures:

1. *Enter the trial balance figures*. The balance of each general ledger account is entered in the appropriate trial balance column of the worksheet. The balances summarize all the transactions for the month before any adjusting entries have been applied.

2. *Enter the adjustments*. After the trial balance figures have been entered and the totals are in agreement, the adjusting entries should be entered in the second pair of columns. The related debits and credits are keyed by letters so that they may be rechecked quickly for any errors. The letters should be in proper sequence, beginning with the accounts at the top of the page.

3. *Extend the trial balance figures and the adjustment figures to either the income statement or balance sheet columns*. The process of extending the balances horizontally should begin with the account at the top of the sheet. The revenue and expense accounts should be extended to the income statements columns; the assets, liabilities, and capital to the balance sheet columns. Each figure is extended to only one of the columns. After the adjusted trial balance column totals have been proved out, then the income statement columns and the balance sheet columns should also prove out.

4. *Total the income statement columns and the balance sheet columns*. The difference between the debit and credit totals in both sets of columns should be the same amount, which represents net income or net loss for the period.

5. *Enter the net income or net loss*. Net income increases capital, so the net income figure should go on the credit side of the balance sheet. Conversely, a net loss decreases the capital, so the net loss figure should go on the debit side of the balance sheet.

You Need to Know ✔

The worksheet is one of the best ways yet developed of avoiding errors in the permanent accounting records. The worksheet also simplifies the work at the end of the period, such as preparing financial statements.

Summary

1. The balances that appear in the first two columns of the worksheet originate from the _____.

2. All changes in accounts appear in the _____ columns of the worksheet.

3. If the total of the debit column of the income statement in the worksheet is larger than the total of the credit column of the income statement, the balance is said to be a _____ for the period.

Answers: 1. ledger; 2. adjustment; 3. net loss

Solved Problems

Solved Problem 8.1 The following selected accounts are taken from the ledger of Casey Mudd. Place indicate which statement—Income Statement (I) or Balance Sheet (B)—the account would appear on and whether the account should be debited (Dr.) or credited (Cr.).

(a) Cash
(b) Accounts Receivable
(c) Accounts Payable
(d) C. Mudd, Capital
(e) C. Mudd, Drawing
(f) Fees Income
(g) Depreciation Expense
(h) Salaries Payable

Solution:

(a) B, Dr. (b) B, Dr. (c) B, Cr. (d) B, Cr. (e) B, Dr. (f) I, Cr. (g) I, Dr. (h) B, Cr.

Solved Problem 8.2 Joe Hurt owns and operates Rent-a-Wreck Company, a used car rental business. The following is a trial balance before the end of the month adjustments.

	Dr.	Cr.
Cash	1,940	
Accounts Receivable	1,575	
Supplies	1,740	
Prepaid Rent	2,900	
Equipment	16,500	
Accounts Payable		1,000
Joe Hurt, Capital		21,650
Joe Hurt, Drawing	2,500	
Rental Income		7,125
Salaries Expense	1,800	
Utilities Expense	540	
Miscellaneous Expense	280	
	29,775	29,775

Listed below are the end of the month adjustments:
   (a) Inventory of supplies at end of month, $975
   (b) Rent for the month, $900
   (c) Depreciation expense for month, $500
   (d) Salaries Payable, $200

Prepare an adjusted trial balance and make the necessary adjusting entries.

Solution:

Account Title	Trial Balance Dr.	Trial Balance Cr.	Trial Balance Adjustments Dr.	Trial Balance Adjustments Cr.	Adjusted Trial Balance Dr.	Adjusted Trial Balance Cr.
Cash	1,940				1,940	
Accounts Receivable	1,575				1,575	
Supplies	1,740			(a) 765	975	
Prepaid Rent	2,900			(b) 900	2,000	
Equipment	16,500				16,500	
Accounts Payable		1,000				1,000
J. Hurt, Capital		21,650				21,650
J. Hurt, Drawing	2,500				2,500	
Rental Income		7,125				7,125
Salaries Expense	1,800		(d) 200		2,000	
Utilities Expense	540				540	
Miscellaneous Expense	280				280	
	29,775	29,775				
Supplies Expense			(a) 765		765	
Rent Expense			(b) 900		900	
Depreciation Expense			(c) 500		500	
Accumulated Depreciation				(c) 500		500
Salaries Payable				(d) 200		200
Total Adjustments			2,365	2,365		
Total Adjusted Trial Balance					30,475	30,475

Adjusting Entries:

(a) Supplies Expense   765
      Supplies   765
(b) Rent Expense   900
      Prepaid Rent   900
(c) Depreciation Expense   500
      Accumulated Depreciation   500
(d) Salaries Expense   200
      Salaries Payable   200

Chapter 9
THE MERCHANDISING COMPANY

IN THIS CHAPTER:

✔ *Introduction*
✔ *Purchases*
✔ *Adjusting Entry Procedures*
✔ *Worksheet Procedures*
✔ *Closing Entries*
✔ *Financial Statement Treatment*
✔ *Conclusion*
✔ *Summary*
✔ *Solved Problems*

Introduction

There are three types of business enterprises that make up the business society:

1. **Service**. Companies and individuals that yield a service to the consumer, such as lawyers, physicians, airlines, etc.

2. **Manufacturing**. Companies that convert raw materials into fin-

ished products, such as housing construction companies and lumber mills.

3. *Merchandising*. Companies that engage in buying and selling finished goods, such as department stores and retail establishments.

This chapter examines the third type, merchandising companies.

Purchases

When the periodic inventory system is used to account for inventory, purchases of merchandise during the period are not debited to the Merchandise Inventory account, but rather are debited to a separate account known as Purchases. This account includes only merchandise bought for resale. Other types of purchases (machinery, furniture, trucks, etc.) that are to be used in the business, rather than sold, are debited to the particular asset account involved and appear in the balance sheet.

Adjusting Entry Procedures

Merchandising (trading) businesses are those whose income derives largely from buying and selling goods rather than from rendering services.

Inventory represents the value of goods on hand at either the beginning or the end of the accounting period. The beginning balance is the same amount as the ending balance of the previous period. Generally, not all purchases of merchandise are sold in the same period, so unsold merchandise must be counted and priced, and its total recorded in the ledger as Ending Inventory. The amount of this inventory is shown as an asset in the balance sheet.

 **Note!**

The amount of goods sold during the period is shown as cost of goods sold in the income statement.

Worksheet Procedures

As discussed previously, the worksheet is usually prepared in pencil on a multicolumn sheet of accounting stationery called analysis paper. On the worksheet, the ledger accounts are adjusted, balanced, and arranged in proper form for preparing financial statements. All procedures can be reviewed quickly, and the adjusting and closing entries can be made in the formal records with less chance of error. Moreover, with the data for the income statement and balance sheet already proved out on the worksheet, these statements can be prepared more readily.

For a typical merchandise business, we may suppose the worksheet to have eight money columns, namely a debit and a credit column for each of four groups of figures: trial balance, adjustments, income statement, and balance sheet. The steps in completing the worksheet are, then, similar to those for a service business (refer to Chapter 8 to review the steps).

Closing Entries

The information for the month-to-month adjusting entries and the related financial statements can be obtained from the worksheet. After the income statement and balance sheet have been prepared from the worksheet for the last month in the fiscal year, a summary account—known as Income Summary—is set up. Then, by means of closing entries, each expense account is credited so as to produce a zero balance, and the total amount of the closed-out accounts is debited to Income Summary. Similarly, the individual revenue  accounts are closed out by debiting, and the total amount is credited to the summary account. Thus, the new fiscal year starts with zero balances in the revenue and expense accounts, though assets, liabilities, and capital accounts are carried forward. Note that the Income Summary balance gives the net income or net loss for the old year. Finally, Income Summary is closed to the Capital account.

Financial Statement Treatment

The Income Statement

The classified income statement sets out the amount of each function and enables management, stockholders, analysts, and others to study the changes in function costs over successive accounting periods. There are three functional classifications of the income statement:

1. *Revenue*. Revenue includes gross income from the sale of products or services. It may be designated as sales, income from fees, and so on, to indicate gross income. The gross amount is reduced by sales returns and by sales discounts to arrive at net sales.

2. *Cost of Goods Sold*. The inventory of a merchandising business consists of goods on hand at the beginning of the accounting period and those on hand at the end of the accounting period. The beginning inventory appears in the income statement and is added to purchases to arrive at the cost of goods available for sale. Ending inventory is deducted from the cost of goods available for sale to arrive at cost of goods sold.

3. *Operating Expenses*. Operating expenses includes all expenses or resources consumed in obtaining revenue. Operating expenses are further divided into two groups. Selling expenses are related to the promotion and sale of the company's product or service. Generally, one individual is held accountable for this function, and his or her performance is measured by the results in increasing sales and maintaining selling expenses at an established level. General and administrative expenses are those related to the overall activities of the business, such as the salaries of the president and other officers. When preparing income statements, list expenses from highest to lowest except Miscellaneous, which is always last, no matter how large the amount may be.

Conclusion

Under the periodic inventory method of inventory calculation, all purchases are recorded in the Purchases account. At the end of the accounting period, the firm takes a physical count of all inventory that is on hand. The cost of the inventory includes the net purchase price plus any cost of transportation. The total cost of purchases is then added to Beginning Inventory to get cost of goods available for sale. The cost of the Ending Inventory is then subtracted from the goods available for sale to get goods available for sale sold. The cost of goods sold is then subtracted from Sales to get gross profit, which is then reduced by operating expenses to determine net income.

Summary

1. Merchandise Inventory (ending) appears as an _____ in the _____ (financial statement).

2. The only account figure that appears on both the income statement and the balance sheet is _____.

3. The beginning balance of Merchandise Inventory would be the same amount as the ending balance of the _____ period.

4. Each of the revenue and each of the expense account balances is closed into the _____ account by means of _____.

5. The accounts with zero balance at the beginning of the year would be those involving _____ and _____.

Answers: 1. asset, balance sheet; 2. Merchandise Inventory; 3. preceding; 4. Income Summary, closing entries; 5. income, expenses

Solved Problems

Solved Problem 9.1 The Mills Company purchased merchandise costing $150,000. What is the cost of goods sold under each assumption below?

	Beginning Inventory	Ending Inventory
(a)	100,000	60,000
(b)	75,000	50,000
(c)	50,000	30,000
(d)	0	10,000

Solution:
To calculate cost of goods sold (CGS), use the following equation:
Beginning Inventory + Purchases − Ending Inventory = CGS

(a) 190,000
(b) 175,000

(c) 170,000
(d) 140,000

Solved Problem 9.2 Compute the cost of goods sold from the following information: Beginning Inventory, $30,000; Purchases, $70,000; Purchase Returns, $3,000; Ending Inventory, $34,000.

Solution:

Beginning Inventory	$30,000
Purchases	$70,000
Less: Purchase Returns	3,000
Net Purchases	$67,000
Goods Available for Sale	$97,000
Less: Ending Inventory	34,000
Cost of Goods Sold	$63,000

Solved Problem 9.3 Prepare an income statement based on the following data.

  (a) Merchandise Inventory, Jan. 1, 2000, $30,000
  (b) Merchandise Inventory, Dec. 31, 2000, $24,000
  (c) Purchases, $66,000
  (d) Sales Income, $103,000
  (e) Purchase Returns, $2,000
  (f) Total expenses, $27,900

Solution:

Sales Income			$103,000
Cost of Goods Sold:			
Beginning Inventory		$30,000	
Purchases	$66,000		
Less: Purchase Returns	2,000	$64,000	
Goods Available for Sale		$94,000	
Less: Ending Inventory		24,000	
Cost of Goods Sold			$ 70,000
Gross Profit			$ 33,000
Total Expenses:			27,900
Net Profit			$ 5,100

Chapter 10
COSTING MERCHANDISE INVENTORY

Introduction

In a merchandising business, inventory is merchandise that is held for resale. As such, it will ordinarily be converted into cash in less than a year and is thus a current asset. In a manufacturing business, there will usually be inventories of raw materials and goods in process in addition to an inventory of finished goods. Since we have discussed the Merchandise Inventory account as it relates to the worksheet, let us now examine how the merchandise inventory amount is calculated.

Determining Inventory: Physical Count

Under the *periodic method*, inventory is physically counted at regular intervals (annually, quarterly, or monthly). When this system is used, credits are made to the Inventory account or to Purchases, not as each sale is made, but rather in total at the end of the accounting period.

To approach the problem of inventory measurement, in order to assign the business cost to each item, three methods of valuation (*FIFO*, *LIFO*, and *weighted average*) have been developed and approved by GAAP (Generally Accepted Accounting Practices). To compare these three methods, the following data will be used in all of the following inventory examples.

Date	Type	Units	Unit Cost	Totals
1/1	Inventory	100	$ 6	$ 600
3/10	Purchase	150	8	1,200
6/6	Purchase	200	9	1,800
10/4	Purchase	250	10	2,500
Available for sale		700		$6,100

It will be assumed that a physical count of inventory on the last day of the accounting period (December 31) showed 320 units on hand. Therefore, 380 units (700 – 320) were sold during the year.

Remember

When using the periodic method of inventory counting, the physical inventory is taken at regular intervals. The credits reducing the Inventory account are made at the end of accounting period, rather than as each sale is made.

Costing Inventory: First-In, First-Out (FIFO)
The first-in, first-out (FIFO) method of costing inventory assumes that goods are sold in the order in which they were purchased. Therefore, the

goods that were bought first (first-in) are the first goods to be sold (first-out), and the goods that remain on hand (ending inventory) are assumed to be made up of the latest costs. Therefore, for income determination, earlier costs are matched with revenue and the most recent costs are used for balance sheet valuation.

This method is consistent with the actual flow of costs, since merchandisers attempt to sell their old stock first. (Perishable items and high-fashion items are examples.) FIFO is the most widely used inventory method of those that will be discussed.

Under FIFO, those goods left at the end of the period are considered to be those received last. Therefore, the 320 units on hand on December 31 would be costed as follows:

Most recent purchase (10/4)	250 units @ $10 =	$2,500
Next most recent purchase (6/6)	70 units @ $ 9 =	630
Ending inventory	320 units	$3,130

The latest cost of the inventory consists of 250 units at $10. However, since the ending inventory consists of 320 units, we must refer to the next most recent purchase of 70 units at $9. Therefore, you could say that the process for determining the cost of the units on hand involves working backward through the purchases until there is a sufficient quantity to cover the ending inventory count. Thus the ending inventory under the FIFO method would be valued and recorded at $3,130.

The costs of goods sold can be determined by subtracting the value of the ending inventory from the total value of the inventory available for sale ($6,100 − $3,130 = $2,970). Since 320 units remain as ending inventory, the number of units sold is 380.

It should be noted that as a method of assigning costs, FIFO may be used regardless of the actual physical flow of merchandise. Indeed, we might say that FIFO really stands for first-price in, first-price out. In a period of rising prices, inflation, the FIFO method will yield the largest inventory value, thus resulting in a larger net income. This situation occurs because this method assigns an inventory cost based on the most recent, higher costs. Conversely, the FIFO method would produce a smaller cost of goods sold, because the earlier, lower costs are assigned to the cost of goods sold.

Note!

Because FIFO results in the most recent charges to inventory, the value of the ending inventory is closer to its replacement cost than under any other method.

Costing Inventory: Last-In, First-Out (LIFO)

The last-in, first-out (LIFO) method of costing inventory assumes that the most recently purchased items are the first ones sold and the remaining inventory consists of the earliest items purchased. In other words, the goods are sold in the reverse order in which they are bought. Unlike FIFO, the LIFO method specifies that the cost of inventory on hand (ending inventory) is determined by working forward from the beginning inventory through purchases until sufficient units are obtained to cover the ending inventory. This is the opposite of the FIFO system. Remember that FIFO assumes costs flow in the order in which they are incurred, while LIFO assumes that costs flow in reverse order from that in which they are incurred.

Under LIFO, the inventory at the end of the period is considered to be merchandise purchased in the first part of the period. Therefore, the 320 units on hand on December 31 would be costed as follows:

Beginning Inventory (1/1)	100 units @ $ 6 =	$ 600
Next purchase (3/10)	150 units @ $ 8 =	1,200
Next purchase (6/6)	70 units @ $ 9 =	630
Ending inventory	320 units	$2,430

Thus, ending inventory under the LIFO method would be valued at $2,430. The cost of good sold is determined by subtracting the value of the ending inventory from the total value of the inventory available for sale ($6,100 – $2,430 = $3,670).

A disadvantage of the LIFO method is that it does not represent the actual physical movement of goods in the business, as most businesses do not move out their most recent purchases. Yet firms favor this method because it does match the most recent costs against current revenue, thereby keeping earnings from being greatly distorted by any fluctuating increases or decreases in prices. Yet it sometimes allows too much maneuvering by managers to change net income. For example, if prices are rising rapidly and a company wishes to pay less taxes for that year, management can buy large amounts of inventory near the end of that period. These  higher inventory costs, because of prices, under LIFO immediately become an expense, and thus result in the financial statement showing a lower net income. Conversely, if the firm is having a bad year, management may want to increase net income to garner favor with stockholders. This can be done by delaying any large purchase of high-cost inventory until the following period by keeping the purchase out of the Cost of Goods Sold section for the current year, and thus avoiding any decrease in net income.

In a rising market, certain tax advantages are gained through LIFO because it yields a lower profit because of its higher cost of goods sold. This can be shown by using the data while assuming sales of $20,000 for the year.

	FIFO	LIFO
Sales	$20,000	$20,000
Cost of Goods Sold		
Goods Available for Sale	$6,100	$6,100
Less: Ending Inventory	3,130	2,430
Cost of Goods Sold	2,970	3,670
Gross Profit	$17,030	$16,330

This information shows LIFO produces (in a rising price market): a lower ending inventory, a higher cost of goods sold, and a lower gross profit. FIFO will produce the opposite.

The IRS will permit companies to use LIFO for tax purposes only if they use LIFO for financial reporting purposes. Thus, if a business uses LIFO for tax purposes, it must also report inventory and income on the same valuation basis in its financial statements, but it is allowed to report an alternative inventory amount in the notes to the financial statements. This is permitted because it affords true financial analysis in comparing, on a similar basis, one business with another. It should be noted that a business cannot change its inventory valuation method any time it chooses. Once a method has been adopted, the business should use the same procedure from one period to the next. If management feels a need to change, permission must be granted by the IRS. The business must then follow specific authoritative guides that detail how the changes should be treated on financial statements.

Costing Inventory: Average Cost Valuation
The average cost valuation system, also known as weighted average, is based on the average cost of inventory during the period and takes into consideration the quantity and the price of the inventory items by assigning the same amount of cost to identical items. In other words, it spreads the total dollar costs of the goods available for sale equally among all the units. The ending inventory is determined by the following procedure:

1. The cost of the total number of units available for sale (beginning inventory plus purchases) is divided by the total units available for sale.

2. The number of units in the ending inventory is multiplied by this weighted average figure.

Date	Type	Units	Unit Cost	Totals
Jan. 1	Inventory	100	$ 6	$ 600
Mar. 10	Purchase	150	$ 8	1,200
June 6	Purchase	200	$ 9	1,800
Oct. 4	Purchase	250	$10	2,500
Available for sale		700		$6,100

Figure 10-1

Referring to the data in Figure 10-1, the cost of the 320 units on hand would be calculated as follows:
1. $6,100 divided by 700 units = $8.71 unit cost.
2. $8.71 multiplied by 320 units on hand = $2,787 ending inventory.
The cost of goods sold is then calculated by subtracting the value of the ending inventory from the total value of the inventory available for sale ($6,100 – $2,787 = $3,313). Because there were 700 units available for sale and 320 units on hand at the end of the period, the number of units sold was determined as 700 – 320 = 380 units.

The average cost method is best used by firms that buy large amounts of goods that are similar in nature and stored in a common place. Grain, gasoline, and coal are good examples of products that could logically be costed under weighted average.

There are some limitations that should be noted in this valuation procedure. Unit cost cannot be related to any physical purchase and does not represent any price changes. In those industries that are greatly affected by price and style change, this method will not yield specific cost determination. Also, the time needed to assemble the data is greater under this method then for FIFO or LIFO, if there are many purchases of a variety of different items bought.

Remember

The three methods for costing inventory are: first-in, first-out (FIFO), last-in, first-out (LIFO), and weighted average cost valuation system.

Comparison of Inventory Methods
The three methods described above of inventory valuation are based on an assumption as to the flow of costs. The FIFO method is based on the assumption that costs flow in the order in which they were incurred; the LIFO method assumes that costs flow in the reverse of the order in which they were incurred; and the weighted average assumes that costs should be assigned to the merchandise inventory based on an average cost per unit. Note that if the costs of all purchases remain the same, the three methods of inventory valuation will yield identical results. As you will realize, prices never stay constant, so each of these three methods will result in a different cost for the ending inventory. Remember that the ending figure is subtracted from the cost of goods available for sale to arrive at the cost of goods sold. Therefore, the net income or loss will vary depending upon the inventory method chosen. Also, the ending inventory on the balance sheet will vary with each method.

Since ending inventory and cost of goods sold are related in the equation

Goods available for sale − Ending inventory = Cost of goods sold

it can be seen that if the ending inventory is *overstated* then the cost of goods sold will be *understated* and net profit *overstated*. Likewise, if inventory is *understated* then cost of goods sold will be *overstated* and net profit *understated*. Clearly, the method chosen for inventory computation can have a marked effect upon the profit of a company. There is no *one* method that is the best, but the firm must consider the following factors to help make the decision:
1. The effect on the income statement and the balance sheet.
2. The effect on taxable income.
3. The effect on the selling price.

The following evaluations can be made concerning the three valuation methods:

FIFO
1. Yields the lowest amount of cost of goods sold (COGS)
2. Yields the highest amount of gross profit
3. Yields the highest amount of ending inventory

 **Note!**

During a period of inflation or rising prices, the use of FIFO will have these effects, but in a declining economy the results will be reversed.

LIFO
1. Yields the highest amount of COGS
2. Yields the lowest amount of gross profit
3. Yields the lowest amount of ending inventory

Weighted Average
Yields results between FIFO and LIFO for all three concepts being reviewed.

Determining Inventory: Estimation

Although a physical inventory is taken once a year, there are occasions when the value of the inventory must be known during the year. When interim financial statements are requested, an inventory amount must be estimated. If no physical count is taken, the amount of inventory must be estimated. Also, in the event of fire or any other casualty, an amount must be reported as a loss. Two of the most popular methods of estimating inventory are the *gross profit method* and the *retail method*.

Gross Profit Method

This method rearranges the Cost of Goods Sold section of the income statement. As stated before, the cost of goods sold formula is:

Beginning Inventory
+ Net Purchases
Goods Available For Sale
− Ending Inventory
Cost of Goods Sold

Note that when you subtract ending inventory from the goods available for sale, the cost of goods sold is determined. Conversely, if you subtract the estimated cost of goods sold from the goods available for sale, the value of the ending inventory will result. The estimated cost of goods sold figure is arrived at by using the past year's gross profit percentage and subtracting the resulting amount from sales.

For example, during the past five years, a company's gross profit averaged 30 percent of sales. If the sales for this interim period are $70,000, the inventory at the beginning of the period is $30,000, and the net purchases are $50,000, you would estimate the ending inventory under the gross profit method as follows:

Beginning Inventory		$30,000
Add: Net Purchases		50,000
Goods Available For Sale		$80,000
Sales	$70,000	
Estimated Gross Profit (30%)	21,000	
Estimated Cost of Goods Sold		49,000
Estimated Ending Inventory		$31,000

This method of estimating ending inventory is also useful for determining casualty losses such as fires, flood, or theft, when such a calamity destroys a company's inventory. It is obvious that a dollar amount must be assigned to the inventory lost before any insurance claim can be made. Although this may appear to be an impossible task, it is possible to build up to the inventory figure.

Retail Inventory Method

The retail inventory method of inventory costing is used by retail businesses, particularly department stores. Department stores usually determine gross profit monthly but only take a physical inventory on an annual basis. The retail inventory method permits a determination of inventory at any time of the year and also produces a comparison of the estimated ending inventory with the physical inventory ending inventory, both at retail prices. This will help to identify any inventory shortages resulting from theft or other causes.

This method, similar to the gross profit method, is used to estimate the dollar cost of the ending inventory when a physical count cannot be done, such as in the case of fire. The procedure for determination under this method is as follows:

1. Beginning inventory and purchases must be recorded at both cost and selling prices.

2. Total goods available for sale are then computed on both bases.

3. Sales for the period are deducted from the goods available for sale at selling price.

4. Ending inventory at selling price is the result of step 3. This amount is then converted to ending inventory at cost by multiplying by the appropriate markup ratio.

The procedure is illustrated in the example below:

		Cost	Selling Price
Step 1.	Beginning inventory	$280,000	$400,000
	+ Net Purchases for period	110,000	180,000
Step 2.	Goods available for sale	$390,000	$580,000
Step 3.	– Net sales for period		340,000
	Ending inventory @ selling price		$240,000

Step 4.   Cost to selling price ratio ($390,000 / $580,000) = 67%
Ending inventory @ cost ($240,000 × 67%) = $160,800

In the above example, the cost percentage is 67%, which means that the inventory and purchases are marked up to yield a gross profit margin of 33%. Certainly not all items in the goods available for sale are marked up by exactly the same percentage, but it is the average. In other words, the retail method will use a percentage that represents an average of markup cost.

Summary Comparison
The major difference between the gross profit method and the retail method is that the former uses the historical gross profit rates, and the latter uses the percentage markup from the current period. The gross profit method uses past experience as a basis, whereas the retail method uses current experience.

The gross profit method is usually less reliable, because past situations may be different from current ones. Remember that both methods are useful because they allow the accountant to prepare interim financial statements more frequently without taking the time to physically count the inventory. However, the annual physical count is necessary.

Summary

1. When inventory is physically counted at the end of an accounting period, we have the _____ method.
2. The _____ inventory method is most commonly used in retail establishments.
3. In a rising market, net income under _____ would be smaller, thus producing a smaller tax.
4. The inventory method based on the concept that the unit of cost of merchandise sold is the average of all expenditures for inventory is known as _____.
5. Of the two methods of estimation, the _____ is less reliable as an indicator of the inventory.

Answers: 1. periodic; 2. periodic; 3. LIFO; 4. weighted average; 5. gross profit method

Solved Problems

Solved Problem 10.1 The inventory information of a product is given below:

Jan. 1	Inventory	12 units	$15
Feb. 16	Purchase	8 units	16
Mar. 4	Purchase	15 units	18
Oct. 15	Purchase	10 units	20

After taking a physical count, we find that we have 14 units on hand. Determine the ending inventory cost by the (a) FIFO method, (b) LIFO method and (c) weighted average.

Solution:

(a) FIFO method

Most recent purchase (10/15)	10 units @ $20 = $200
Next most recent purchase (3/4)	4 units @ $18 = 72
Ending Inventory	14 $272

(b) LIFO method

Beginning Inventory	12 units @ $15 = $180
Next Purchase	2 units @ 16 = 32
Ending Inventory	14 $212

(c) Weighted Average

$778 / 45 units = $17.29 per unit
14 units on hand times $17.29 per unit = $242.06 ending inventory

Solved Problem 10.2 Determine the gross profit under the (a) LIFO and (b) FIFO assumptions, given the following information:

Sales	$40,000
Goods available for sale	12,000
Ending Inventory (under LIFO)	6,500
Ending Inventory (under FIFO)	3,500

Solution:

(a) LIFO method

Sales		$40,000
Cost of Goods Sold:		
Goods Available	$12,000	
Less Ending Inventory	<u>6,500</u>	
Cost of Goods Sold		<u>5,500</u>
Gross Profit		$34,500

(b) FIFO method

Sales		$40,000
Cost of Goods Sold:		
Goods Available	$12,000	
Less Ending Inventory	<u>3,500</u>	
Cost of Goods Sold		<u>8,500</u>
Gross Profit		$31,500

Chapter 11
PRICING
MERCHANDISE

Trade Discounts

When merchandise is offered for sale by manufacturers or wholesalers, a *list* or *catalog price* is set for each item. This represents the price that the ultimate consumer will pay for the item.

74

Rather than printing separate prices for each of the potential purchasers, the seller gives the various classes of buyers a separate discount sheet, detailing the discount offered to his or her class of purchaser. Thus, the trade discount is not a true discount but is considered to be an *adjustment of the price.*

The use of a list or catalog price also cuts down on printing. If the seller wishes to change the price offered to the wholesaler or retailer, a revised discount schedule, using the original list or catalog price, would be sent. The list or catalog price also provides the retailer with a suggested selling price for the item. The price the buyer pays for the item is computed by multiplying the list or catalog price by the discount rate and then subtracting this discount from the list or catalog price.

Chain Discounts

Rather than give varying increasing single discounts to different classes of purchasers, some companies use chain discounts. These have the advantage of appearing to be higher and emphasizing to the buyer the fact that she or he receives *more* than one discount.

When using chain discounts, there are two methods that may be used to compute the net cost price:

1. Determine a single equivalent discount and then proceed to compute the net cost price. This method is also useful for companies that wish to compare varying discount policies of competing companies. To compute an equivalent discount, *multiply* the complements of each of the discounts (100 percent – discount) together and subtract the result from 100 percent. For example, the single discount equivalent of 10 percent and 20 percent is computed as:

Step 1	(100% – 10%) multiplied by (100% – 20%)
Step 2	0.90 multiplied by 0.80 = 0.72
Step 3	Equivalent discount = 100% – 72% = 28%

2. The net cost price can be computed directly by *multiplying* the list price by the complement of each of the discounts in the series. It does not make any difference in what order the discounts are arranged.

Cash Discounts

Cash discounts are an inducement offered to the buyer to encourage payment of a bill within a specified period of time. They tend to narrow the gap between the time of sale and the time of collection, which can become a source of cash flow difficulties for the seller.

Cash discounts are referred to as *terms* and may appear on a bill as 2/10, net 30, where, 2 equals the percent of the discount, 10 equals the number of days within which the buyer must pay in order to qualify for the discount, and net 30 equals the number of days at which payment must be made in full.

Some companies offer a varied cash discount depending on when payment is made, for example, 2/10, 1/20, net 30. This means that the company offers a 2 percent discount if the buyer pays within 10 days; if he or she pays after 10 days, but within 20 days of purchase, he or she gets a 1 percent discount; the net amount is due within 30 days.

Although in most cases the cash discount period is computed from the "invoice" or purchase date, the date may also be computed from either the date of *receipt of goods* (ROG) or starting with the *end of the month* (EOM). ROG is primarily used when there is a significant gap between the date of the sale and the delivery date. EOM is used primarily as a convenience with traditional end-of-month billing practices followed by most companies.

You Need to Know

When both trade and cash discounts are offered, the cash discount is computed *after* the trade discount has been taken.

Markup

In order to make a profit, each company must sell its products for more than they cost. The difference between cost and selling price is referred to as *markup*.

Markup is generally expressed in terms of a percentage:

$$Percent = (Percentage\ /\ Base)$$

where percent in the above equation equals the markup percent, percentage equals the markup, and base equals the selling price or cost.

Remember

Three different kinds of discounts that sellers offer purchasers of their goods are: trade discounts, chain discounts, and cash discounts.

Selling Price as a Basis: Computing Percent Markup

In order to use the percent markup to compute either the cost or the selling price, the selling price formula must be reexamined in terms of percents. It should be noted that the base is 100 percent. For example, a book selling for $8 has a markup percent of 25 percent. The cost of the book would be $6.

Cost as a Basis

When cost is used as a base for markup percent, it is sometimes referred to as a *markon*. It has the advantage of expressing clearly the fact that the price increase is added *directly* to its basis (cost). In order to compute the percent markup, the equation would be:

$$Percent\ markup = (\$\ markup\ /\ cost)$$

For example, a ball point pen that sells for $6 cost $4. The percent markup based on cost would be 50 percent.

In order to compute the selling price from either the cost or the markup, you once again must look at the formula for selling price from the point of view of percents. The cost (basis) is 100 percent. For example, a tie that costs $10 has a markup of 30 percent on cost would have a selling price of $13.

Markdowns

Once the price of an item has been established, there is no guarantee that this will represent the ultimate selling price. Downward adjustments of the selling price are often necessary to induce customers to buy. These are referred to as *markdowns*. The seller is in effect forced, perhaps because of overstocking or too high a selling price, to abandon the original price. Markdowns take the form of *direct price reductions*.

Turnover—Ratios for Inventory

The firm's investment in inventory also has a direct effect on its working capital. Excess inventory means that funds are tied up in inventory that could be used more profitably elsewhere. Also, additional costs are being incurred for storage, insurance, and property taxes, not to mention the danger of a price decline and obsolescence of goods.

Whenever any consideration is given to pricing and profit planning, it is important to consider the merchandise inventory turnover. This is the number of times the average inventory is sold during a year. The turnover shows how quickly the inventory is moving. Assuming that the company maintains a reasonable inventory for its type of business, a high turnover rate indicates that only a relatively small profit need be added to the price of each item to maintain a high profit overall. Turnover is also a good indication of the amount of working capital that needs to be tied up in inventory at one time.

Merchandise inventory turnover can be computed from the cost of goods sold section of the income statement. It should be noted, however, that the turnover is an annual rate and should not be computed from interim financial statements. Merchandise inventory turnover is calculated by taking the cost of goods sold divided by the average merchandise inventory. The average merchandise inventory is defined as beginning inventory plus ending inventory divided in half.

Note!

In a retail business, such as a department store, turnover may effectively be computed either by departments or by classes of items.

Number of Days' Sales in Inventory

The relationship between inventory and cost of goods sold can also be expressed as the number of days' sales in inventory. In this ratio, the inventory at the end of the year is divided by the average daily cost of goods sold. The latter figure is determined by dividing the cost of goods sold by 365. The number of days' sales in inventory provides a rough measure of the length of time required to buy, sell, and then replace the inventory.

Summary

1. An adjustment of the retail price is known as a _____.

2. A substitute for varying increasing single discounts to different classes of purchases is referred to as a _____.

3. An inducement offered to the buyer to encourage payment of his or her bill within a specific period of time is called a _____.

4. The difference between cost and selling price is referred to as _____.

5. In order to give consideration to pricing and profit planning, it is important to consider the _____.

Answers: 1. trade discount; 2. chain discount; 3. cash discount; 4. markup; 5. merchandise inventory turnover

Solved Problems

Solved Problem 11.1 Equipment of $400 is sold to a retailer at a 25 percent trade discount. What is the retailer's cost?

Solution:

Trade Discount: $400 times 25% = $100

List Price	$400
Trade Discount	100
Net Cost	$300

Solved Problem 11.2 If transportation of $20 were added to the purchase in Solved Problem 11.1, what would be the net cost?

Solution:

Net cost: $300 + 20 (Transportation costs) = $320

Transportation costs are added to the net cost of the item and are not subject to trade discounts.

Solved Problem 11.3 Julie Pearman bought $800 of supplies for her company, less chain discounts of 30 percent and 20 percent. (a) What is the single equivalent discount? (b) What is the net cost to the company?

Solution:

(a) (100% − 30%) times (100% − 20%) = 70% times 80% = 56%
    Single equivalent discount = 44% (100% − 56%)
(b) $800 times 44% = $352
    Net cost = $448 ($800 − $352)

Solved Problem 11.4 Determine the last day allowable for a company to take advantage of the full discount.

Term	Date of Order	Delivery Date
(a) 2/10, n/30	June 4	June 8
(b) 2/10, 1/15, n/30	June 4	June 8

(c) 2/10, n/30, ROG   June 4   June 8
(d) 2/10, n/30, EOM   June 4   June 8

Solution:

(a) June 14
(b) June 14 (full); June 19 (partial)
(c) June 18
(d) July 10

Chapter 12
NEGOTIABLE INSTRUMENTS

IN THIS CHAPTER:

Introduction

A large portion of all business transactions are credit transactions. One way of extending credit is by the acceptance of a promissory note, a contract in which one person (the maker) promises to pay another per-

son (the payee) a specific sum of money at a specific time, with or without interest. A promissory note is used for the following reasons:

1. The holder of a note can usually obtain money by taking the note to the bank and selling it (discounting the note).

2. The note is a written agreement of a debt and is better evidence than an open account.

3. The note facilitates the sale of merchandise on long-term or installment plans.

For a note to be negotiable, it must meet the requirements of the Uniform Negotiable Instrument Law. This legislation states that the instrument:

1. The note must be in writing and signed by the maker.

2. The note must contain an order to pay a definite sum of money.

3. The note must be payable to order on demand or at a fixed future time.

Methods of Computing Interest

For the sake of simplicity, interest is commonly computed on the basis of a 360-day year divided into 12 months of 30 days each. Two widely used methods are the cancellation method and the 6 percent, 60-days method.

The Cancellation Method
Consider a note for $400 at 6 percent for 90 days. The principal is the face amount of the note ($400). The rate of interest is written as a fraction: 6/100. The time, if less than a year, is expressed as a fraction by dividing the number of days the note runs by the number of days in a year: 90/360. Thus

$$\text{Interest} = \$400 \times (6/100) \times (90/360) = \$6$$

The 6 Percent, 60-Days Method
The 6 percent, 60-days Method is a variation of the cancellation method, based on the fact that 60 days, or 1/6 of a year, at 6 percent is equivalent to 1 percent, so that the interest is obtained by shifting the decimal point of the principal two places to the left.

Determining Maturity Date

The maturity days are the number of days after the note has been issued and may be determined by:

1. Subtracting the date of the note from the number of days in the month in which it was written.

2. Adding the succeeding full months (in terms of days), stopping with the last full month before the number of days in the note are exceeded.

3. Subtracting the total days of the result of steps 1 and 2 above from the time of the note. The resulting number is the due date in the upcoming month.

If the due date is expressed in months, the maturity date can be determined by counting that number of expressed months from the date of writing.

 **Note!**

The two most widely used methods of calculating interest are the cancellation method and the 6 percent, 60-days method.

Accounting for Notes Payable and Notes Receivable

A promissory note is a note payable from the standpoint of the maker; it is a note receivable from the standpoint of the payee.

Notes Payable

A note payable is a written promise to pay a creditor an amount of money in the future. Notes are used by a business to purchase items, settle an open account, or borrow money from a bank.

1. Purchase items

Assume that Spencer bought office equipment costing $2,000 by giving a note.

Office Equipment	2,000	
Notes Payable		2,000

2. Settle an open account

There are times when a note is issued in settlement of an account payable. Assume that the Julie Agency bought merchandise from the Josh Corporation for $500 and at the end of the month, the account balance remained in full. If the Julie Agency is unable to pay, they may issue a note to the Josh Corporation for the $500 account payable, converting the account payable into a note payable. Note that the Julie Agency still owes the debt to Josh Corporation. However, it now becomes a different form of obligation, as it is a written, signed promise in the form of a note payable.

3. Borrow money from a bank

On occasion, businesses find it necessary to borrow money by giving a note payable to a bank. Frequently, banks require the interest be paid in advance. This is accomplished by deducting the amount of the interest from the principal when the loan is made and is known as *discounting a note payable*. The proceeds will be that amount of money that the maker of the note receivable receives after the discount has been taken from the principal.

Notes Receivable

A note received from a customer is an asset because it becomes a claim against the buyer for the amount due.

Assume that Howard Cogan owes David Smith $400 and gives him a 90-day, 15 percent note in settlement. Mr. Cogan still owes the debt, but his obligation is of a different type now. On Mr. Smith's books the entry is:

Notes Receivable	400	
Accounts Receivable		400

Only the principal ($400) is recorded when the note is received, since it represents the amount of the unpaid account. The interest is not due until the date of collection, 90 days later. At that time, the interest earned will be part of the entry recognizing the receipt of the proceeds from the note:

Cash	415	
Notes Receivable		400
Interest Income*		15

*Interest = $400 \times (15/100) \times (90/360) = 15

Discounting

The negotiability of a note receivable based upon its maturity value, enables the holder to receive cash from the bank before the due date. This is known as *discounting*.

Once the interest to be paid has been determined, the procedure for discounting a note is quite simple. The *maturity value* of a note is:

1. Maturity value = face of note + interest income

where the face is the principal and interest income is computed as before. The holder of a note may discount it at the bank prior to its due date. He or she will receive the maturity value, less the discount, or interest charge imposed by the bank for holding the note for the unexpired portion of its term. In other words,

2. Discount = maturity value × discount rate × unexpired time, and

3. Net Proceeds = maturity value − discount.

For example, Mr. Ed holds a $400, 90-day, 12 percent note written by Mr. Bill on April 10. It is discounted at 12 percent on May 10. The interest on the note amounts to $12. Hence:

1. Maturity value = $400 + $12 = $412

Since at the time of discounting, Mr. Ed has held the note for only 30 days, the bank will have to wait 60 days until it can receive the maturity value. The discount charge is then

2. Discount = $412 × (12/100) × (60/360) = $8.24

and Mr. Ed receives

3. Net proceeds = $412 − $8.24 = $403.76

 **Note!**

The bank's discount rate happened to be equal to the interest rate, but this need not always be the case.

Dishonored Notes Receivable

If the issuer of a note does not make payment on the due date, the note is said to be dishonored. It is no longer negotiable, and the amount is charged back to Accounts Receivable. The reasons for transferring the dishonored notes receivable to the Accounts Receivable accounts are that the Notes Receivable account is then limited to current notes that have not yet matured and the Accounts Receivable account will then show the dishonoring of the note, giving a better picture of the transaction.

For example, a $500, 60-day, 12 percent note written by F. Saltzman was dishonored on the date of maturity. The entry is:

Accounts Receivable, F. Saltzman   510
    Notes Receivable   500
    Interest Income   10

Observe that the interest income is recorded and is charged to the customer's account.

When a payee discounts a note receivable, he or she creates a contingent (potential) liability. This occurs because there is a possibility that the maker may dishonor the note. Bear in mind that the payee has already received payment from the bank in advance of the maturity date. The payee is, therefore, contingently liable to the bank to make good on the amount (maturity value) in the event of default by the maker. Any protest fee arising from the default of the note is charged to the maker of the note and is added to the amount to be charged against his or her account.

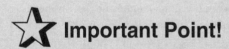 **Important Point!**

The concept known as discounting permits the negotiability of a note receivable based upon its maturity value to enable the holder to receive cash from the bank before the due date.

Recording Uncollectible Accounts

Businesses must expect to sustain some losses from uncollectible accounts and should therefore show on the balance sheet the *net amount of accounts receivable*, the amount expected to be collected, rather than the gross amount. The difference between the gross and net amounts represents the estimated *uncollectible accounts*, or bad debts. These expenses are attributed to the year in which the sale is made, though they may be realized at a later date.

There are two methods of recording uncollectible accounts, the *direct write-off method* and the *allowance method.*

Direct Write-Off Method

In small businesses, losses that arise from uncollectible accounts are recognized in the accounts *in the period in which they become uncollectible.* Under this method, when an account is deemed uncollectible, it is written off the books by a debit to the expense account, Bad Debt Expense, and a credit to the individual customer's account and to the controlling account.

For example, if Bill Anderson's $300 account receivable, dated May 15, 200X, was deemed uncollectible in January of 20XX, the entry in 20XX would be:

Bad Debt Expense	300
Accounts Receivable, Bill Anderson	300

Allowance Method

As stated before, one of the fundamentals of accounting is that revenue be matched with expenses in the same year. Under the direct write-off method example above, the loss was not recorded until a year after the revenue had been recognized. The allowance method does not permit this. The income statement for each period must include all losses and expenses related to the income earned *in that period.* Therefore, losses from uncollectible accounts should be deducted in the year in which the sale is made. Since it is impossible to predict which particular accounts will not be collected, an adjusting entry is made, usually at the end of the year.

For example, assume that in the first year of operation, a firm has estimated that $2,000 of accounts receivable will be uncollectible. The adjusting entry would be:

Bad Debt Expense	2,000	
Allowance for Bad Debt		2,000

The credit balance of Allowance for Bad Debt (contra asset) appears on the balance sheet as a deduction from the total amount of Accounts Receivable:

Accounts Receivable	$30,000
Less: Allowance for Bad Debt	2,000
	$28,000

The $28,000 will become the estimated realizable value of the accounts receivable at that date. The bad debt expense will appear as an operating expense in the income statement.

Computing Uncollectible Accounts

There are two generally accepted methods of calculating the amount of uncollectible accounts. One method is to use a flat percentage of the net sales for the year. The other method takes into consideration the ages of the individual accounts at the end of the fiscal year.

Percentage of Sales Method
Under the percentage of sales method, a fixed percentage of the total sales on account is taken. For example, if charge sales were $200,000 and experience has shown that approximately 1 percent of such sales will become uncollectible at a future date, the adjusting entry for the bad debt account would be:

Bad Debt Expense	2,000	
Allowance for Bad Debt		2,000

The same amount is used whether or not there is a balance in the Allowance for Bad Debt account. However, if any substantial balance should accumulate in the allowance account, a change in the percentage figure would become appropriate.

Balance Sheet Method

Under the balance sheet method, every account is "aged"; that is, each item in the balance is related to the sale date. The further past due the account, the more probable it is that the customer is unwilling or unable to pay. A typical analysis is shown below.

Age of Account	A/R Balance	Est. % Uncollectible	Amount
1–30 days	$ 8,000	1%	$ 80
31–60 days	12,000	3%	360
61–90 days	6,000	5%	300
91–180 days	3,000	20%	600
Over 180 days	920	50%	460
	$29,920		$1,800

The calculated allowance for uncollectible accounts ($1,800 above) is reconciled at the end of the year with the actual balance in the allowance account, and an adjusting entry is made. The amount of the adjusting entry must take into consideration the balance of the Allowance for Bad Debt account. The percentage of sales method does not follow this procedure.

Recovery of Uncollectible Accounts

If a written-off account is later collected in full or part (a *recovery of bad debts*), the write-off will be reversed for the amount received.

For example, after his account has been written off, Mr. Andrew pays his account in full. The reversing entry to restore his account will be:

Accounts Receivable, John Andrew	600	
Allowance for Bad Debt		600

A separate entry will then be made in the cash receipts journal to record the collection, debiting Cash $600 and crediting Accounts Receivable, John Andrew. If a partial collection was made, the reversing entry should be made for the amount recovered.

Summary

1. The holder of a note can usually obtain money by taking it to a bank and _____ it.
2. The face of a note plus the interest due is known as _____.
3. A written promise to pay a creditor an amount of money in the future is known as a _____.
4. The two methods of recording uncollectible accounts are the _____ method and the _____ method.
5. There are two methods of calculating the amount of uncollectible accounts. They are the _____ method and the _____ method.

Answers: 1. discounting; 2. maturity value; 3. note payable; 4. direct write-off, allowance; 5. percentage of sales, balance sheet

Solved Problems

Solved Problem 12.1 Below is an example of a note receivable.

July 1, 2002

I, Megan MacLaren, promise to pay Concord, Inc., $900, 90 days from date, at 14 percent interest.

Megan MacLaren

(a) Who is the maker of the note? (b) Who is the payee of the note? (c) What is the maturity date of the note? (d) What is the maturity value of the note?

Solution:

(a) Megan MacLaren; (b) Concord, Inc.; (c) September 29; (d) $931.50

Solved Problem 12.2 Determine the interest on the following notes: (a) $750 principal, 14 percent interest, 96 days; (b) $800 principal, 12 percent interest, 90 days.

Solution:

(a) $750	14%	60 days	$17.50
	14%	30 days	8.75
	14%	6 days	1.75
		96 days	$28.00
(b) $800	12%	60 days	$16.00
	12%	30 days	8.00
		90	$24.00

Solved Problem 12.3 A $4,000, 90 day, 14 percent note receivable in settlement of an account, dated June 1, is discounted at 14 percent on July 1. Compute the proceeds of the note.

Solution:

Principal	$4,000.00
Interest Income (90 days, 14%)	140.00
Maturity Value	$4,140.00
Discount (60 days, 14% of maturity value)	96.60
Proceeds	$4,043.40

Solved Problem 12.4 What are the entries needed to record the information in Solved Problem 12.3 (a) on June 1? (b) on July 1?

Solution:

(a) Notes Receivable	4,000.00	
Accounts Receivable		4,000.00
(b) Cash	4,043.40	
Interest Income		43.40
Notes Receivable		4,000.00

Solved Problem 12.5 Bill's Bank received a $20,000, 90 day, 14.5 percent note from Sun Town Company on account, dated November 1. Sun Town paid the note on the due date. (a) Show the entries for this transaction. (b) Show the adjusting entry assuming December 31 is the last day of the accounting period?

Solution:

(a) Nov. 1	Notes Receivable		20,000	
		Accounts Receivable		20,000
Jan. 30	Cash		20,725	
		Interest Income		725
		Notes Receivable		20,000
(b) Dec. 31	Interest Receivable		483.33	
		Interest Income		483.33 *

*$20,000 times 14.5% times 1/6 (November and December)

Chapter 13
CONTROLLING CASH

In This Chapter:

- ✔ *Introduction*
- ✔ *Controlling Cash Receipts*
- ✔ *Controlling Cash Disbursements*
- ✔ *Controlling Cash Balances*
- ✔ *Bank Statements*
- ✔ *Petty Cash*
- ✔ *Summary*
- ✔ *Solved Problems*

Introduction

In most firms, transactions involving the receipt and disbursement of cash far outnumber any other kinds of transactions. Cash is, moreover, the most liquid asset and most subject to theft and fraud. It is, therefore, essential to have a system of accounting procedures that will maintain adequate control over cash.

Cash is a medium of exchange and includes such items as currency, coin, demand deposits, saving deposits, petty cash funds, bank drafts, cashier's checks, personal checks, and money orders.

Controlling Cash Receipts

In a very small business the owner can maintain control through personal contact and supervision. In a larger firm, this kind of direct intervention must be replaced by a system of internal control, exercised though accounting reports and records.

The specific controls applied to cash receipts are as follows:

1. All receipts should be banked promptly.

2. Receipts from cash sales should be supported by sales tickets.

3. Accountability should be established each time cash is transferred.

4. Persons receiving cash should not make disbursements of cash, record cash transactions, or reconcile bank accounts.

Controlling Cash Disbursements

Payments must be made only by properly authorized persons, equivalent value be received, and documents must support the payment adequately. Following are specific internal controls relating to cash disbursements:

1. All disbursements, except petty cash, should be made by prenumbered check.

2. Vouchers and supporting documents should be submitted for review when checks are signed.

3. Persons who sign checks should not have access to cash receipts, should not have custody of funds or record cash entries, and should not reconcile bank accounts.

Controlling Cash Balances

The basic principle of separation of duties is evident in the specific controls for cash balances:

1. Bank reconciliations should be prepared by persons who do not receive cash or sign checks.

2. Bank statements and paid checks should be received unopened by the person reconciling the account.

3. All cash funds on hand should be closely watched and surprise counts be made at intervals.

If the requirement that all cash receipts be banked is followed, then it is clear that the monthly bank statement can be made a powerful control over cash balances.

Bank Statements

Checks

A business opens a checking account to gain the privilege of placing its deposits in a safe place and the ability also to write checks. When an account is opened, each person who is authorized to write checks on that account must sign a signature card. The bank keeps the signature card on file and compares it when checks are submitted. The check becomes a written notice by the depositor directing the bank to deduct a specific sum of money from the checking account and to pay that amount to the person or company written on the check. A check involves three parties:

1. Drawer—the firm that writes the check
2. Drawee—the bank on which the check is drawn
3. Payee—the person or company to whom the check is paid.

Checks offer several advantages. The checkbook stubs provide a record of the cash paid out, while the canceled checks provide proof that money has been paid to the person legally entitled to it. Also, the use of checks is the most convenient way of paying bills, because checks can safely be sent through the mail.

Remember

If a check is lost or stolen, the depositors can request the bank not to pay (a stop order).

Endorsements

When a check is given to the bank for deposit, the depositor signs the check to show that he or she accepts responsibility for the amount of that check. The depositor's signature is known as an *endorsement*. This endorsement transfers the ownership of the check and guarantees to the individual that the depositor will guarantee its payment. Different kinds of endorsements serve different needs.

1. *Blank endorsements*. A blank endorsement consists only of the name of the endorser. Its disadvantage lies in the fact that a lost or stolen check with a blank endorsement may be cashed by the finder or thief.

2. *Endorsement in full*. Endorsement in full states that the check can be cashed or transferred only on the order of the person named in the endorsement.

3. *Restrictive endorsement*. A restrictive endorsement limits the receiver of the check as to the use he or she can make of the funds collected. Usually this type of endorsement is done when checks are prepared for deposit.

Reconciliation

Each month, the bank forwards to the depositor a statement of his or her account showing the beginning balance, all the deposits made and other credits, any checks paid and other charges (debits), and the ending balance.

Included in this envelope with the statement are the paid or canceled checks and any other deductions or additions to the account. A deduction may be a debit memorandum for bank service charges; an addition may be a credit memorandum for the proceeds of a note collected by the bank for the depositor.

Usually the balance of the bank statement and the balance of the depositor's account will not agree. To prove the accuracy of both records, the reconciling differences have to be found and any necessary entries made. The reconciling items will fall into two broad groups: those on the depositor's books but not recorded by the bank, and those on the bank statement but not on the depositor's books. The statement used to reconcile this difference is known as the bank reconciliation sheet.

Items on Books But Not Found on Bank Statement

Deposits in Transit. These comprise cash receipts recorded by the company but too late to be deposited. The total of such deposits is added to the bank balance.

Outstanding Checks. These are checks issued by the depositor but not yet presented to the bank for payment. The total of these checks is deducted from the bank balance.

Errors. Bookkeeping errors may be made in recording amounts of checks, for example a transposition of figures. The item should be added to the balance if overstated and deducted if understated.

Items on Bank Statements But Not on Books

Service charges. The bank generally deducts amounts for bank services. The exact amount is usually not known by the depositor until the statement is received. The amount should be deducted from the book balance.

NSF (not sufficient funds) checks. NSF checks have been deposited but cannot be collected due to insufficient funds in the account of the drawer of the check. The bank then issues a debit memorandum charging the depositor's account. The amount should be deducted from the book balance.

Collections. The bank collects notes and other items for a small fee. The bank then adds the proceeds to the account and issues a credit memorandum to the depositor. Often there are unrecorded amounts at the end of the month. The amounts should be added to the book balance.

Bank Errors. Bank errors should not be entered on the books. They should be brought to the attention of the bank and corrected by the bank. Journal entries used in accounting for the differences between the bank balance and the depositor's balance is known as a *bank reconciliation*.

Petty Cash

To eliminate the necessity of writing checks in very small amounts, it is customary to maintain a petty cash fund from which small disbursements are made. Examples are postage, delivery expense, telegrams, and so on.

Each disbursement from the petty cash fund should be accounted for by a receipt. If no bill is presented, the one responsible for the fund should prepare a receipt and have the payee sign it. This is known as a *petty cash voucher*. The face of the voucher should contain the following data:

1. Receipt number
2. Date of Disbursement
3. Name of payee
4. Amount of the expenditure
5. Purpose for which the expenditure was made
6. Account affected by the expenditure
7. Signature of payee.

Under the *imprest* system, a fund is established for a fixed petty cash amount, and this fund is periodically reimbursed by a single check for amounts expended. The steps in setting up and maintaining the petty cash fund are as follows:

1. An estimate is made of the total of the small amounts likely to be disbursed over a short period, usually a month. A check is drawn for the estimated total and put into the fund. The only time an entry is made in the petty cash account is to establish the fund initially, unless at some later time it is determined that this fund must be increased or decreased.

2. The individual in charge of petty cash usually keeps the money in a locked box along with petty cash vouchers. The petty cash voucher, when signed by the recipient, acts as a receipt and provides information concerning the transaction. As each payment is made, the voucher is entered in the petty cash record under the heading, "Payments."

3. The amount paid is then distributed to the account affected.

4. The columns are totaled in order to determine the amount chargeable to each account.

5. A check is then drawn in an amount equaling the total amount disbursed.

6. When the check is cashed, the money is replaced in the fund to restore it to the original amount.

7. Each amount listed in the distribution section of the petty cash fund is entered as a debit to the individual expense. The total amount of the check is credited to Cash.

8. Proof of petty cash is obtained by counting the currency and adding the amounts of all the vouchers in the box. The total should agree with the amount in the ledger for the petty cash fund. If it does not, the entry in the cash disbursements journal recording the reimbursement of the petty cash fund will have to include an account known as *Cash Short and Over*. A cash shortage is debited and a cash overage is credited to this account. Cash Short and Over is closed out at the end of the year in to the Income Summary account and is treated as a general expense or miscellaneous income.

Summary

1. The most liquid asset and also the one most subject to theft and fraud is _____.

2. A check involves three parties: the _____, who writes the check;

the _____, the bank on which it is drawn; and the _____, the person to whom it is to be paid.

3. The signature on the back of a check showing that the individual accepts responsibility for that amount is known as an _____.

4. Under the _____, a fund is established for a fixed petty cash amount that is reimbursed by a single check for amounts expended.

5. If a proof of petty cash is impossible, the account _____ will have to be used.

Answers: 1. cash; 2. drawer, drawee, payee; 3. endorsement; 4. imprest system; 5. Cash Short and Over

Solved Problems

Solved Problem 13.1 In order to produce equal adjusted balances for A&J Company, indicate whether each of items 1–8 below should be:

(a) Added to the bank statement balance
(b) Deducted from the bank statement balance
(c) Added to the depositor's balance
(d) Deducted from the depositor's balance
(e) Exempted from the bank reconciliation statement

1. Statement includes a credit memo, representing the collection of the proceeds of a note left at the bank.

2. A credit memo representing the proceeds of a loan made to A&J Company by the bank.

3. Deposits in transit.

4. Seven outstanding checks were not recorded on the statement.

5. A customer's check that A&J Company had deposited was returned with "nonsufficient funds" stamped across the face.

6. The bank erroneously charged someone else's check against A&J's account.

7. A&J Company was credited on the bank statement with the receipt from another depositor.

8. A $96 check was erroneously recorded in A&J's check stubs as $69.

Solution:

1. (c); 2. (c); 3. (a); 4. (b); 5. (d); 6. (a); 7. (b); 8. (d)

Solved Problem 13.2 At the close of the day, the total cash sales as determined by the sales registers were $1,580. However, the total cash receipts amounted to only $1,570. The error cannot be located at the present time. What entry should be made to record the cash sales for the day?

Solution:

Cash	1,570	
Cash Short and Over	10	
Sales Income		1,580

Solved Problem 13.3 Of the following transactions involving the bank reconciliation statement, which ones necessitate an adjusting entry on the depositor's books? Show the adjusting entries.

(a) Outstanding checks of $3,000 did not appear on the statement.
(b) The last 2 days' deposited receipts, $2,850, did not appear on the bank statement.
(c) The depositor's check for $120 for supplies was written in her records as $210.
(d) Bank service charge, $4.

Solution:

(c) Cash	90	
Supplies		90
(d) Service Charge Expense	4	
Cash		4

Chapter 14
PAYROLL

In This Chapter:

✔ *Gross Pay*
✔ *Deductions from Gross Pay*
✔ *The Payroll System*
✔ *Recording the Payroll*
✔ *Summary*
✔ *Solved Problems*

Gross Pay

The pay rate at which employees are paid is generally arrived at through negotiations between the employer and the employees. The employer, however, must conform with all applicable federal and state laws. One law requires that workers, excluding salaried workers or workers in industries such as hotels and restaurants, be compensated at one and one-half times their regular pay for hours worked over 40. Gross pay for wage earners is generally computed by using an individual time card.

Deductions from Gross Pay

Federal Withholding Taxes

Federal income taxes are withheld from gross pay on a pay-as-you-go-system. The amount to withhold from each employee is determined after consideration of four factors:

1. the amount of gross pay
2. the taxpayer's filing status (married or single)
3. the number of exemptions claimed by the taxpayer, and
4. the payroll period.

The employee's filing status and number of exemptions claimed is determined by referring to Form W-4, filled out by each employee when he or she began to work. An employee is entitled to one personal exemption and one for his or her spouse and each dependent.

Social Security Taxes (Federal Insurance Contributions Act—FICA)

The FICA tax helps pay for federal programs for old age and disability benefits, Medicare, and insurance benefits to survivors. During the working years of an employee, funds will be set aside from his or her earnings. When the employee's earnings cease because of disability, retirement, or death, the funds are made available to his or her dependents or survivors.

A combined rate of 7.65 percent (subject to change as enacted by Congress) is imposed on both the employee and the employer. Thus, the total is 15.30 percent. The 7.65 percent is broken down into two parts: 6.2 percent for old-age, survivors, and disability insurance (OASDI) and 1.45 percent for hospital insurance (Medicare). The OASDI rate (6.2 percent) applies to wages within the OASDI wage base, which is $87,000 for 2003. The Medicare rate (1.45 percent) applies to all wages earned during the year regardless of the amount earned.

You Need to Know

The amounts withheld for either income tax or FICA represent a liability for the employer, as these amounts are required to be remitted to the Internal Revenue Service. The same is true for other withholdings, such as retirement contributions or union dues.

State and Local Withholding Taxes

Most states and some cities impose a tax on the gross earnings of each residential employee. These taxes are also withheld from the employee's pay and turned over periodically by the employer to the appropriate agency.

All the deductions discussed so far have been mandatory. Often, through agreement with the employer, amounts will be withheld for retirement plans, union dues, savings bonds, insurance, and other deductions.

 **Note!**

An employee is entitled to one personal exemption and one for his or her spouse and each dependent (child) when filing their Form W-4.

The Payroll System

The payroll system generally consists of input data (time cards), a payroll register (to compute the payroll each pay period), individual earnings cards (a separate record for each employee), paychecks, and a system for recording both the payroll and the related employer taxes with appropriate liabilities.

Individual Time Card

Although the overall payroll is recorded in a payroll register, it is also necessary to know both the earnings and the deductions for each employee separately. These individual records facilitate the preparation of required governmental reports and assist the employer in maintaining control over payroll expenditures. They also act as convenient references to basic employee information such as earnings to date, exemptions, filing status, and employee classification. Information from the payroll register is posted immediately after recording the payroll to the individual earnings cards.

Payroll Register

A payroll register is a specially designed form used at the close of the payroll period to summarize and compute the payroll for the period. Although the design of this form may vary slightly depending on desired information and the degree of automation, most contain the same basic information. The five main sections of the payroll register include:

1. Computation of gross earning

2. Taxable earnings, used as a reference to compute FICA tax withheld or paid by the employer and unemployment tax payable by the employer.

3. Deductions from gross pay—a place is provided for each tax withheld and for miscellaneous deductions.

4. Net pay. This is the employee's take home pay. This may be checked by adding the total of deductions to the net pay.

5. Gross salaries charged to specific accounts.

Recording the Payroll

The payroll is generally recorded initially in the general journal. Since the payroll register is the input for the entry, it is generally totaled for the payroll period and proved before any entry is made.

Employers are required to pay unemployment taxes to both the federal and state governments. Although the typical state unemployment tax rate is 5.4 percent, rates vary depending on the state, nature of the business, and the employer's experience with unemployment. The official federal unemployment tax rate is 6.2 percent. As long as the employer is up to date on the state tax, the employer is allowed an automatic credit of 5.4 percent no matter what rate the employer actually pays. The effective federal unemployment rate is therefore 0.8 percent.

Summary

1. The amount of federal income tax withheld from a person is based on the individual's _____ and _____.

2. Form _____ will yield information pertaining to the number of exemptions an employee is filing.

3. The payroll _____ is the input for the payroll entry.

4. The two types of payroll taxes imposed on the employer are _____ and _____.

5. The one tax that is paid by the employee and matched by the employer is _____.

Answers: 1. filing status, number of exemptions; 2. W-4; 3. register; 4. FICA, unemployment; 5. FICA

Solved Problems

Solved Problem 14.1 How many exemptions are permitted to be claimed on Form W-4 in the following cases:

(a) Taxpayer and spouse
(b) Taxpayer, spouse, and two children
(c) Taxpayer, spouse, and mother she fully supported

Solution:

(a) 2; (b) 4; (c) 3

Solved Problem 14.2 Judy Bogan worked 44 hours during the first week in February of the current year. The pay rate is $9 per hour. Withheld from her wages were FICA; federal income tax, $47; hospitalization, $7.20. Prepare the necessary payroll entry.

Solution:

Salaries Expense	414*	
FICA—Social Security Payable		25.67
FICA—Medicare Payable		6.00
Federal Income Tax Payable		47.00
Hospitalization Payable		7.20
Salaries Payable		328.13

*40 hours times $9 = $360 (regular pay)
4 hours times $13.50 = $54 (overtime pay)
$360 + $54 = $414 (total pay)

Solved Problem 14.3 Based on the information in Solved Problem 14.2, what is the entry to record the employer's payroll tax if it is assumed the state tax rate is 4 percent and the federal unemployment rate is 0.8 percent? (Prior to payroll) earnings to date = $5,100.

Solution:

Payroll Tax Expense	51.54	
FICA—Social Security Payable		25.67
FICA—Medicare Payable		6.00
Federal Unemployment Insurance Payable		3.31
State Unemployment Insurance Payable		16.56

Chapter 15

PROPERTY, PLANT, AND EQUIPMENT: DEPRECIATION

IN THIS CHAPTER:

✔ *Fixed Assets*
✔ *Depreciation and Scrap Value*
✔ *Depreciation Methods*
✔ *Comparison of Methods*
✔ *Summary*
✔ *Solved Problems*

Fixed Assets

Tangible assets that are relatively permanent and are needed for the production or sale of goods or services are termed *property, plant, and equipment (PP&E)*, or *fixed assets*. These assets are not held for sale in the ordinary course of business. The broad group is usually separated into classes according to the physical characteristics of the items, for example land, buildings, machinery and equipment.

The cost of PP&E includes all expenditures necessary to put the asset into position and make it ready for use.

Depreciation and Scrap Value

Though it may be long, the useful life of a fixed asset is limited. Eventually the asset will lose all productive worth and will possess only salvage value or scrap value. The accrual basis of accounting demands a period-by-period matching of costs against derived revenues. Hence the cost of a fixed asset (over its scrap value) is distributed over the asset's entire estimated lifetime. This spreading of the cost over the periods that receive benefits is known as *depreciation.*

To determine depreciation expense for a fixed asset, we need the following information:

1. *Cost*. The total purchase price of the item, including its initial cost, transportation, sales tax, installation and any other expense to make it ready for use.

2. *Estimated Useful Life*. The projected life during which the business expects the asset to function. This may be expressed in years, miles, units of production, or any other measure appropriate.

3. *Residual Value*. Also called scrap or salvage value, residual value is the estimated value of the asset when it is fully depreciated. When subtracted from the cost of the asset, it produces the "depreciable cost."

Depreciation decreases the fixed asset's book value and also decreases capital. Depreciation is considered an operating expense of the business. It may be recorded by an entry at the end of each month or at the end of the year, usually depending on the frequency of preparing financial statements. Fixed assets are recorded at cost and remain at that figure as long as they are held. The depreciation taken to date is shown as a credit in the contra asset account Accumulated Depreciation and is deducted from the asset account on the balance sheet.

An offset (contra) account is an account with a credit balance that is offset against an asset account to produce the correct balance sheet book value. The offset account appears in the general ledger directly after its companion account. Generally, every depreciable asset has its own count and an accumulated depreciation account. To determine th book, or carrying, value, the accumulated depreciation accou tracted from the asset account.

There is one exception to the above considerations: land. This fixed asset is nondepreciable; it is usually carried on the books permanently at cost.

 **Note!**

Three pieces of information are needed to calculate depreciation on any asset: total cost, estimated useful life, and residual (or scrap) value.

Depreciation Methods

The depreciable amount of a fixed asset—that is, cost minus scrap value—may be written off in different ways. The amount may be spread evenly over the years, as in the straight-line method, or it may be accelerated. Two accelerated methods are the double-declining balance and the sum-of-the-years'-digits method. These methods provide for larger amounts of depreciation in the earlier years. Repairs, on the other hand, are generally lower in earlier years, so the total cost of depreciation and repairs should be about the same each year. The units-of-production method bases depreciation each period on the amount of output.

Straight-Line (SL)
The straight-line method is the simplest and most widely used depreciation method. Under this method, an equal portion of the cost of the asset is allocated to each period of use. The periodic charge is expressed as:

$$\frac{\text{Cost} - \text{scrap value}}{\text{Useful life (in years)}} = \text{Annual Depreciation Charge}$$

For example, if the cost of a machine is $17,000, its scrap value is $2,000 and its estimated useful life is 5 years, depreciation can be calculated as follows:

$$\frac{\$17,000 - \$2,000}{5 \text{ years}} = \$3,000 \text{ per year}$$

The entry to record the depreciation would be:

Depreciation Expense, Machinery	3,000	
Accumulated Depreciation, Machinery		3,000

In order to have sufficient documentation for an asset's depreciation, a schedule should be prepared showing the asset's cost, depreciation expense, accumulated depreciation, and most important of all, its book value. *Book value* is the balance of an asset's cost less its accumulated depreciation to date.

Book value should not be confused with market value. The book value is the difference between cost and accumulated depreciation. Market value is what the asset can actually be sold for on a given date.

As an asset is used, accumulated depreciation increases and book value decreases. In the final year of the assets useful life, book value is the same as scrap value. At this point, the asset is said to be fully depreciated.

If an asset is held for more than half a month, that month is counted. If it is held for less than 15 days in a month, that month is not counted. An asset bought on or before the 15th of the month is considered to be in use and therefore can be depreciated for the entire month. If it is bought on or after the 16th, it cannot be depreciated for that month and depreciation will begin in the next month.

Units of Production (UOP)

Units of production depreciation is based on an asset's usage. This can be expressed in:

1. Units produced
2. Hours consumed
3. Mileage driven

This method is used when an asset's usage varies from year to year.

Units Produced. Under the first variation of the UOP method, a fixed amount of depreciation is allocated to each unit of output produced by the machine. The per-unit depreciation expense is multiplied by the number of units produced in each accounting period. This depreciation method accurately reflects the depreciation expense for the asset because it is based on the number of units produced in each period. Depreciation per unit is computed in two steps:

1. $$\frac{\text{Cost of asset} - \text{scrap value}}{\text{Total estimated units of output}} = \text{Depreciation per unit}$$

2. Units produced × unit depreciation = Annual depreciation expense

For example, if the cost of a machine is $17,000, its scrap value is $2,000 and its total estimated units produced during its lifetime is 300,000, then the depreciation is calculated as follows (assuming the following facts):

First year production	25,000 units
Second year production	30,000 units

$$\frac{\$17,000 - \$2,000}{300,000} = \$.05 \text{ depreciation per unit}$$

Year 1: 25,000 units × $.05 = $1,250
Year 2: 30,000 units × $.05 = $1,500

Hours Used. In the second variation of UOP, a fixed amount of depreciation is allocated, based on the number of hours the machine is used.

For example, the depreciation for the following machines in the first year using the straight-line method and the UOP hours of usage method is:

	Machine A	Machine B
Cost	$22,000	$22,000
Scrap Value	$ 2,000	$ 2,000
Estimated Life	5 years	5 years
	(18,000 hours)	(18,000 hours)

Machine A was in use for 3,000 hours in the first year
Machine B was in use for 1,000 hours in the first year

Straight Line Depreciation = $4,000 annual depreciation expense*
*($22,000 − $2,000) / 5 years = $4,000

UOP hours of usage = $1.11 annual depreciation expense*
*($22,000 − $2,000) / 18,000 hours = $1.11

Machine A=3,000 hours × $1.11 = $3,330 1st year depreciation expense
Machine B=1,000 hours × $1.11 = $1,110 1st year depreciation expense

The difference between the first-year depreciation using the straight-line method and that using the UOP method is considerable. Under the UOP method, machine B's limited use results in its having one-third the depreciation expense of machine A. Under the straight-line method, both machines carry the same depreciation expense, regardless of use. In this case, UOP is the more logical choice for reporting depreciation because it more accurately matches expense against periodic income.

Mileage Driven. Under the third variation of UOP depreciation, instead of using time to calculate depreciation, the number of miles driven are the "units." The depreciation expense per mile will remain constant over the life of the truck, and will be multiplied by the actual miles the truck is driven in each accounting period.

For example, a truck costing $24,000 with a salvage value of $4,000 has an estimated useful life of 80,000 miles. If, in the first year, it is driven 18,000 miles, depreciation is calculated as follows:

$$\frac{\$24,000 \ (cost) - \$4,000 \ (salvage \ value)}{80,000 \ total \ estimated \ miles} = \$.25 \ per \ mile$$

18,000 (miles driven) × $.25 = $4,500 1st year depreciation expense

Depreciation Expense, Truck	4,500	
Accumulated Depreciation, Truck		4,500

Double-Declining Balance
Double-declining balance is an accelerated method of depreciation because a greater amount of depreciation expense is taken in the early years of an asset's life and less is taken in later years. This method is preferred for the following reasons:

1. Technology can make an asset obsolete or inadequate before the asset wears out.

2. Most plant assets decline in value more quickly in their early years than in later years.

3. Often, an asset contributes most to a business during its first years.

4. The expenditure for equipment is made at the beginning of the asset's life.

5. It is good accounting practice to charge more depreciation in the early years of an asset's useful life.

The double-declining balance method (DDB) produces the highest amount of depreciation in earlier years. It does not recognize scrap value. Instead, the book value of the asset remaining at the end of the depreciation period becomes the scrap value. Under this method, the straight-line rate is doubled and applied to the declining book balance each year. Many companies prefer the double-declining balance method because of the faster write-off in the earlier years when the asset contributes the most to the business and when the expenditure was actually made. The procedure is to apply a fixed rate to the declining book value of the asset each year. As the book value declines, the depreciation becomes smaller.

For example, a $17,000 asset is to be depreciated over 5 years. The double-declining balance rate is thus 40 percent per year.

Year	Book Value at Beginning of Year	Rate	Depreciation for Year	Book Value at End of Year
1	$17,000	40%	$6,800	$10,200
2	10,200	40%	4,080	6,120
3	6,120	40%	2,448	3,672
4	3,672	40%	1,469	2,203
5	2,203	40%	881	1,322

The $1,322 book value at the end of the fifth year becomes the scrap value. If however, a scrap value of $2,000 had been estimated, the depreciation for the fifth year would be $203 ($2,203 − $2,000) instead of $881.

The date of purchase should also be considered. Up to this point it has been assumed that the equipment was purchased at the beginning of the year, which is usually not the case. Therefore a change in the computation for the first partial year is needed.

Sum-of-the-Years'-Digits (SYD)

The fourth method of computing depreciation is sum-of-the-years'-digits. Like DDB, it is an accelerated method that allows more depreciation expense to be recorded in the early years of an asset's life and less in the later years. Like DDB, depreciation expense declines over the life of the asset, but unlike DDB, it declines by the same amount each year.

To determine depreciation expense under SYD, the asset's cost (minus scrap value) is multiplied by a fraction. The numerator of the fraction is the years remaining in the asset's life, but in reverse order. It changes each year. The denominator is the sum of all the digits making up the life of the asset. It remains constant.

For example, if a machine costs $17,000, has a scrap value of $2,000, and an estimated life of 5 years. The depreciable amount is $17,000 − $2,000 = $15,000. To find the fraction of this amount to be written off each year, proceed as follows: the numerator of the fraction for the first year would be 5 (years in reverse). The denominator of the fraction would be 15, the sum of the year's digits (5 + 4 + 3 + 2 + 1 = 15). To determine the depreciation for the first year, multiply $15,000 by (5/15). The current year depreciation is $5,000.

Partial-Year Depreciation

If an asset is purchased during the year rather than at the beginning, each full year's depreciation must be allocated between the two fiscal years affected to assure accurate reporting and accounting. The two fiscal years affected are the first year and the final year of depreciation.

Comparison of Methods

Once you know the four methods of depreciation, the next question is how to select the one that's most appropriate. Under generally accepted accounting principles (GAAP), businesses are encouraged to match the income an asset produces against its expense. This can be accomplished by selecting the correct depreciation method.

Of the four depreciation methods discussed earlier, three are compared in the table below. It is assumed that over a 5-year lifetime the asset was in operation for the following numbers of hours: 1,800, 1,200, 2,000, 1,400, 1,600. Cost of asset, $17,000; scrap value, $2,000.

YEAR	SL	UOP	DDB
1	$ 3000	$ 3375	$ 6800
2	3000	2250	4080
3	3000	3750	2448
4	3000	2625	1468
5	3000	3000	204
Total	$ 15,000	$ 15,000	$ 15,000

Based upon the above table, we can conclude the following:

1. If the asset is expected to generate income evenly over an extended period of time, the *straight-line method* should be used.

2. If the asset will produce a different number of units each year, or if the machine may wear out early, the *units-of-production method* is preferable because it is based upon the usage rather than time.

3. If the asset is expected to generate high income in its early years, the *double-declining balance method* should be used because it will generate greater depreciation expense in its earlier years, as it can be matched with the early period's higher revenues. Like the sum-of-the-years'-digits, this accelerated depreciation method reduces tax liability in the early years, making more cash available for the asset's purchase.

Summary

1. The market value of a fixed asset at the end of its service is known as a _____.

2. The uniform distribution of depreciation over the life of the asset is known as the _____ method.

3. The _____ method is used to write off the asset based on a series of fractions.

4. The method that produces the largest amount of depreciation in the earlier years, then rapidly declines, is known as the _____ method.

5. When income produced by an asset is the same each year, the recommended method of depreciation is _____.

6. When use rather than time is the key factor, _____ is the preferred method of depreciation.

Answers: 1. scrap value; 2. SL; 3. SYD; 4. DDB; 5. SL; 6. UOP

Solved Problems

Solved Problem 15.1 Hacol Company acquired an asset on January 1, 2003, at a cost of $38,000, with an estimated useful life of 8 years and a salvage value of $2,000. What is the annual depreciation based on:

(a) the straight-line depreciation method?
(b) the double-declining-balance method?
(c) the sum-of-the-years'-digits method?

Solution:

(a) Cost $38,000
    Scrap Value   2,000
    Depreciable Cost $36,000

Year 1: $36,000 / 8 years = $4,500 depreciation
Year 2: $36,000 / 8 years = $4,500 depreciation

(b) 2 times (100% / 8 years) = 25% per year

Year 1: $38,000 times 25% = $9,500 depreciation
Year 2: ($38,000 − $9,500) times 25% = $7,125 depreciation

(c) Sum of the years' digits = 36 (8+7+6+5+4+3+2+1)

Year 1: (8 / 36) times $36,000 = $8,000 depreciation
Year 2: (7 / 36) times $36,000 = $7,000 depreciation

Solved Problem 15.2 A truck was purchased on January 1, 2000, for $8,500, with an estimated scrap value of $500. It will be depreciated over 8 years using the straight-line method. Show how the Truck account and the related Accumulated Depreciation account would appear on the balance sheet on (a) December 31, 2000; (b) December 31, 2001.

Solution:

(a) Truck $8,500
     Less: Accumulated Depreciation   1,000 $7,500

(b) Truck $8,500
      Less: Accumulated Depreciation   2,000 $6,500

Solved Problem 15.3 A machine was purchased for $28,000 and had an estimated scrap value of $4,000. What would the year-end entry be if the units-of-production method was used, and it had an estimated life of 32,000 hours? In the first year of operation, it used 7,200 hours.

Solution:

Depreciation Expense, Machine   5,400
      Accumulated Depreciation, Machine   5,400

($28,000 – $4,000) / 32,000 hours = 0.75 times 7,200 hours = $5,400

Solved Problem 15.4 Equipment costing $9,600, with an estimated scrap value of $1,600, was bought on July, 1, 1999. The equipment is to be depreciated by the straight-line method for a period of 10 years. The company's fiscal year is January through December. Show the journal entry to record the equipment's cost on the balance sheet for December 1999.

Solution:

Equipment $9,600
Less: Accumulated Depreciation   400 $9,200

($9,600 – $1,600) divided by 10 years = $800 depreciation per year
1/2 year (July 1 to Dec.31) times $800 per year = $400

Chapter 16
THE PARTNERSHIP

IN THIS CHAPTER:

✔ *Characteristics*
✔ *Formation of the Partnership*
✔ *Division of Net Income and Loss*
✔ *Admission of a New Partner*
✔ *Liquidation of a Partnership*
✔ *Summary*
✔ *Solved Problems*

Characteristics

According to the Uniform Partnership Act, a partnership is "an association of two or more persons to carry on as co-owners of a business for profit." Generally speaking, partnership accounting is like that for the sole proprietorship, except with regards to owner's equity. The partnership uses a capital account and a drawing account for each partner. The partnership has the following characteristics:

1. *Articles of copartnership*. Good business practice calls for a written agreement among the partners that contains provisions on the formation of the partnership, capital contributions of each partner, profit and

loss distribution, admission and withdrawal of partners, withdrawal of funds, and dissolution of business.

2. *Unlimited liability*. All partners have unlimited liability and are individually responsible for debts incurred by the partnership. The debts of the business can be satisfied not only by the assets of the partnership but also by the personal assets of the partners.

3. *Co-ownership of property*. All property invested in the business by the partners, as well as that purchased with the partnership's funds, becomes the property of all partners jointly. Therefore, each partner has an interest in the partnership in proportion to his or her capital balance, rather than a claim against specific assets.

4. *Participation in profits and losses*. Profits and losses are distributed among the partners according to the partnership agreement. If no agreement exists, profit and losses must be shared equally.

5. *Limited life*. A partnership may be dissolved by bankruptcy, death of a partner, mutual agreement, or court order.

Formation of the Partnership

When a partnership is formed, each partner's capital account is credited for his or her initial investment, and the appropriate asset account is debited. If noncash assets are invested, these should be recorded at an agreed amount.

 **Note!**

If liabilities are to be assumed by the partnership, they are credited to the respective liability accounts.

Division of Net Income and Loss

Partnership profits and losses may be divided in any manner the partners may agree upon. In general, a partner may be expected to share in proportion to the amount of capital and/or services he or she contributes. In the absence of a clear agreement, the law provides that all partners share equally, regardless of the differences in time devoted or capital contributed.

Below are outlined the principal methods for profit and loss distribution:

Fixed or Capital Basis
Profits and losses are generally divided equally in a fixed ratio or in a ratio based on the amounts of capital contributed by the partners.

Interest Basis
Under this method, each partner is paid interest on his or her capital investment, and the remaining net income is divided in a fixed ratio or on some other basis. Thus, a partner's share depends on his or her capital investment.

Salary Basis
The partners may agree to give recognition to contributions in the form of services, while the remaining net income may be divided equally or in a fixed ratio.

Salary-Plus-Interest Basis
Here, services rendered to the business and capital contribution jointly determine the income division. Each partner gets a salary, and, at the same time, interest on capital. If any balance remains, it is divided in an agreed ratio.

You Need to Know

When the partnership lacks a clear agreement establishing the division of net income or loss, the law provides that all partners share equally, regardless of the differences in time devoted or capital contributed.

Admission of a New Partner

The Uniform Partnership Act states that a partner may dispose of part or all of his or her interest in the firm without the consent of the remaining partners.

The individual who purchases the interest receives the selling partner's rights to share in income and expense. However, this purchaser is not a full partner, since he or she will have no vote or right to participate in partnership activities unless he or she is admitted to the firm.

Admission by Purchase of Interest

When the incoming partner purchases an interest from another partner, he or she pays the purchase price directly to the old partner. The only change required in the partnership's books is an entry transferring capital from the old partner's account to the account established for the new partner. Assets and liabilities of the business are not affected.

Admission by Contribution of Assets

The new partner may contribute assets to the partnership, thus increasing both the assets and the capital of the firm.

In some cases, when a new partner is admitted, assets may first have to be revalued or goodwill recognized in order to bring the capital accounts into line with current values. This process is known as revaluation of assets. The book values of certain assets of the partnership must be adjusted before they agree with current prices. The net amount of the revaluation is then transferred to the capital accounts of the old partners according to their income division agreement. If it appears that a number of assets need revaluation, whether to  higher or lower figures, the adjustments may be made in a temporary account, *Asset Revaluation*, which will subsequently be closed to the partners' capital accounts.

If a firm has the ability to earn more than the normal rate on its investment (because of a favorable location, established reputation, management skills, or better products or services), goodwill may be indicated, and an incoming partner may be charged for it. If so, the goodwill account is debited, while the old partners' accounts are credited in the ratios set up by the articles of partnership. On the other hand, if goodwill is created by the incoming partner, the goodwill account is debited, and the new partner's capital account credited.

Liquidation of a Partnership

If the partners of a firm decide to discontinue the operation of the business, several accounting steps are necessary:

1. The accounts are adjusted and closed.
2. All assets are converted to cash.
3. All creditors are paid in full.
4. Any remaining cash is distributed among the partners according to the balances in their capital accounts (and not according to their profit and loss ratios).

Summary

1. Partnership and sole proprietorship accounting are alike except in _____.

2. If profits and losses are not to be distributed equally, the basis of distribution must be stated in the _____.

3. In order to reflect higher current prices, certain assets of the partnership will be debited, with the corresponding credit to _____.

4. When a partnership decides to go out of business, the process of selling the assets, paying the creditors, and distributing the remaining cash to the partners is known as _____.

5. The final distribution of cash to the partners is based on their _____.

Answers: 1. owner's equity; 2. partnership agreement; 3. asset revaluation; 4. liquidation; 5. capital

Solved Problems

Solved Problem 16.1 Henderson and Erin have decided to form a partnership. Henderson invests the following assets (shown at their agreed upon value) and he also transfers liabilities to the new firm.

Henderson's Accounts	Value
Cash	$17,500
Accounts Receivable	7,000
Merchandise Inventory	10,000
Equipment	4,200
Accounts Payable	3,500
Notes Payable	3,600

Erin agrees to invest $26,000 in cash. Record (a) Henderson's investment; (b) Erin's investment.

Solution:

(a) Cash	17,500	
Accounts Receivable	7,000	
Merchandise Inventory	10,000	
Equipment	4,200	
Accounts Payable		3,500
Notes Payable		3,600
Henderson, Capital		31,600

(b) Cash	26,000	
Erin, Capital		26,000

Solved Problem 16.2 Adams, Bentley, and Carson have capital balances of $30,000, $25,000, and $20,000, respectively. Adams devotes 75% of his time; Bentley, 50% time; and Carson, 25% time. Determine their participation in net income of $37,500 if income is divided (a) in the ratio of capital investments; (b) in the ratio of time worked.

Solution:

(a) Total capital is $75,000. Hence:

Adams ($30,000 / $75,000) times $37,500 = $15,000
Bentley ($25,000 / $75,000) times $37,500 = $12,500
Carson ($20,000 / $75,000) times $37,500 = $10,000

(b) The ratio is 3:2:1. Hence:

Adams (3/6) times $37,500 = $18,750
Bentley (2/6) times $37,500 = $12,500
Carson (1/6) times $37,500 = $ 6,250

Solved Problem 16.3 The capital accounts in the partnership of Frank and John are $57,500 and $87,500, respectively. The partnership agreement calls for a 15% interest on their capital accounts and the remaining sum to be shared equally. Net income for the year is $30,000. Show the division on net income.

Solution:

	Frank	John
Interest on Capital		
Frank, $57,500 times 15%	$8,625	
John, $87,500 times 15%		$13,125
Balance ($30,000 – 21,750)	$4,125	$ 4,125
divided equally		
Totals	$12,750	$17,250

Chapter 17
THE
CORPORATION

In This Chapter:

- ✔ *Characteristics*
- ✔ *Corporate Terminology*
- ✔ *Advantages of the Corporate Form*
- ✔ *Disadvantages of the Corporate Form*
- ✔ *Equity Accounting for the Corporation*
- ✔ *Common Stock*
- ✔ *Preferred Stock*
- ✔ *Issue of Stock*
- ✔ *Book Value*
- ✔ *Earnings Per Share*
- ✔ *Bond Characteristics*
- ✔ *Funding by Stock Versus Funding by Bonds*

✔ *Summary*
✔ *Solved Problem*

Characteristics

In essence, the corporation is an artificial being, created by law and having a continuous existence regardless of its changing membership. The members are the stockholders; they own the corporation but are distinct from it. As a separate legal entity, the corporation has all the rights and responsibilities of a person, such as entering into contracts, suing and being sued in its own name, and buying, selling, or owning property.

Corporate Terminology

The *stockholders*, as owners of the business, have the right:
1. to vote (one vote for every share of stock held)
2. to share in profits
3. to transfer ownership
4. to share in the distribution of assets in the case of liquidation.

The *board of directors* is elected by the stockholders within the framework of the articles of incorporation. The board's duties include the appointing of corporate officers, determining company policies, and the distribution of profits.

A *share of stock* represents a unit of the stockholders' interest in the business. The par value of a share is an arbitrary amount established in the corporation's charter and printed on the face of each stock certificate. It bears no relation to the *market value*, that is, the current purchase or selling price. There are several categories of stock shares:

1. *Authorized shares* are shares of stock that a corporation is permitted to issue (sell) under its articles of incorporation.

2. *Unissued shares* are authorized shares that have not yet been offered for sale.

3. *Subscribed shares* are shares that a buyer has contracted to purchase at a specific price on a certain date. The shares will not be issued until full payment has been received.

4. *Treasury stock* represents shares that have been issued and later reacquired by the corporation.

5. *Outstanding stock* represents shares authorized, issued, and in the hands of stockholders. (Treasury stock is not outstanding, as it belongs to the corporation and not to the stockholders.)

Advantages of the Corporate Form

The corporate form of business in the United States, when compared to the sole proprietorship or partnership, has several important advantages:

1. *Limited Liability of stockholders*. Each stockholder is accountable for the amount he or she invests in the corporation. If the company should fail, the creditors cannot ordinarily look beyond the assets of the corporation for settlement of their claims.

2. *Ready transfer of ownership*. Ownership of a corporation is evidenced by stock certificates; this permits stockholders to buy or sell their interests in a corporation without interfering with the management of the business. Through the medium of organized exchanges, millions of shares of stock change hands each day.

3. *Continued existence*. The death or incapacity of a partner may dissolve a partnership, but the corporation's existence is independent of the stockholders.

4. *Legal entity*. The corporation can sue and be sued, make contracts, buy and sell in its own name. This is in contrast to the sole proprietorship, which must, by law, use individual names in all legal matters.

5. *Ease of raising capital*. Advantages 1 and 2 make the corporation an attractive investment for stockholders. Compare this to the partnership, where capital raising is restricted by the number of partners, the amounts of their individual assets, and the prospect of unlimited liability.

Disadvantages of the Corporate Form

Although the corporate form of business has the advantages listed above, it also has some disadvantages, such as the following:

1. *Taxation*. The corporation must pay federal income taxes in the same manner as an individual, and this results in double taxation of corporate income. Double taxation develops first from the taxing of the net

profits and second from that portion of the profits distributed to the stockholders as individual income.

2. *Cost of organization*. The corporation must secure state approval and legal assistance in forming this type of ownership. Requirements vary from state to state, but all states require (a) a minimum number of stockholders, (b) a minimum amount of capital, and (c) a payment of incorporation fees and taxes. The legal fees involved may run to thousands of dollars in large firms and must be added to the costs of state fees and taxes.

3. *Legal restrictions*. The charter of the corporation of a state is the basis of the corporation's transactions and permits it to engage in only those activities that are stated or implied in the document. If the corporation wishes to operate in another state, it must either incorporate in that state also or pay a tax to the state.

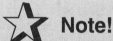 **Note!**

The corporation is the most restricted form of business ownership.

Equity Accounting for the Corporation

Accounting for the corporation is distinguished from accounting for the sole proprietorship or the partnership by the treatment of owner's (stockholder's) equity, which, in the corporation, is separated into paid-in capital and retained earnings. The reason for this separation is that most states prohibit corporations from paying dividends from other than retained earnings. Paid-in capital is further divided, and so we have three major capital accounts:

1. *Capital Stock*. This account shows the par value of the stock issued by the corporation.

2. *Additional Paid-in Capital*. Amounts paid in beyond the par value of stock.

3. *Retained Earnings*. The accumulated earnings arising from profitable operation of the business.

Common Stock

If a corporation issues only one class of stock, it is known as *common stock*, with all shares having the same rights. The ownership of a share of common stock carries with it the right to:

1. Vote in the election of directors and in the making of certain important corporate decisions.

2. Participate in the corporation's profits.

3. Purchase a proportionate part of future stock issues.

4. Share in assets upon liquidation.

Preferred Stock

In order to appeal to a broader market, the corporation may also issue preferred stock. This class of stock does not ordinarily carry voting rights (although such rights are sometimes conferred by a special provision in the charter); however, as its name implies, this stock does take preference over common stock in several respects.

1. *Prior claim against earning*. The board of directors has the power to declare and distribute dividends to the stockholders. In such distributions, the claims of preferred stock are honored before those of common stock. However, the amount of dividends paid to preferred stock is usually placed on the amount paid to common stock. From an accounting viewpoint, the priority in receiving dividends constitutes the most important benefit of preferred stock.

2. *Prior claim to assets*. If, upon liquidation of a corporation, the assets that remain after payment of all creditors are not sufficient to return the full amount of the capital contribution of preferred and common stockholders, payment must first be made to preferred stockholders. Any balance would then go to common stockholders.

Preferred stock may also carry the following options:

1. *Call privilege*. The issuing company will have the right to redeem (call) the stock at a later date for a predetermined price. This call price would be in excess of the original issue price, such as 105 percent of par value.

2. *Conversion privilege*. The stockholders, at their option, may convert preferred stock into common stock. This might be done if the corporation's common stock should become more desirable than the preferred stock because of large earnings.

You Need to Know

Two types of stock that a corporation can offer are common and preferred. All shares of common stock carry a voting right where preferred stock does not ordinarily carry voting rights. Although, preferred stock takes preference over common stock on claims against earnings or claims against assets.

Issue of Stock

Issue at Par

When a corporation is organized, the charter will state how many shares of common and preferred stock are authorized. Often more stock is authorized than is intended to be sold immediately. This will enable the corporation to expand in the future without applying to the state for permission to issue more shares. When stock is sold for cash and issued immediately, the entry to record the security has the usual form: Cash is debited, and the particular security is credited. A corporation may accept property other than cash in exchange for stock. If this occurs, the assets should be recorded at fair market value, usually as determined by the board of directors of the company.

Issue at a Premium or a Discount

The market price of stock is influenced by many factors, such as:

1. Potential earning power.
2. General business conditions and other prospects.
3. Financial condition and earnings record.
4. Dividend record.

Stock will be sold at a price above par if investors are willing to pay the excess, or premium. The premium is not profit to the corporation but rather part of the investment of the stockholders. If the purchaser will not pay par value, the corporation may issue stock at a price below par.

Remember

The difference between par value and the lower price is called the *discount*.

Book Value

The book value per share of stock is obtained by dividing the stockholders' equity amount by the number of shares outstanding. It thus represents the amount that would be distributed to each share of stock if the corporation were to be dissolved.

Individual book values for common and preferred stock are defined by separating the stockholders' equity amount into two parts and dividing each part by the corresponding number of shares. All premiums and discounts, as well as retained earnings or deficits, go to common stock only.

Earnings Per Share

To find earnings per share (EPS), take the net profit after taxes, less any preferred dividends. This will equal the earnings available for common stockholders. Divide by the number of shares of common stock outstanding to arrive at EPS:

$$EPS = \frac{\text{earnings available for common stockholders}}{\text{number of shares of common stock outstanding}}$$

Bond Characteristics

A corporation may obtain funds by selling stock or by borrowing through long-term obligation. An issue of bonds is a form of long-term debt in which the corporation agrees to pay interest periodically and to repay the principal at a stated future date.

Bond denominations are commonly multiples of $1,000. A bond issue normally has a term of 10 or 20 years, although some issues may have longer lives. The date at which a bond is to be repaid is known as the maturity date. In an issue of serial bonds, the maturity dates are spread in a series over the term of the issue. This relieves the corporation from the impact of total payment at one date.

Funding by Stock Versus Funding by Bonds

The major differences between stocks and bonds may be summarized as follows:

Stocks

    1. Representation—Ownership in the corporation

    2. Inducement to Holders—Dividends

    3. Accounting Treatment—Dividends are a distribution of profits; stocks are equity

    4. Repayment—By selling in the market at any time

Bonds

    1. Representation—A debt of the corporation

    2. Inducement to Holders—Interest

    3. Accounting Treatment—Interest is an expense; bonds are a long-term liability

    4. Repayment—On a predetermined date

Summary

    1. The rights to vote and to share in the profits of the company rest with the _____.

    2. The greatest disadvantage of the corporate form of business is the _____ on income.

    3. The profit and loss of the corporation is recorded in the _____ account.

    4. To achieve a broader market and a more attractive issue price, preferred stock may _____ in profits beyond the specified rate.

    5. The amount paid in excess of par by a purchaser of newly issued stock is called a _____, whereas the amount paid below par is known as a _____.

Answers: 1. stockholders; 2. tax; 3. retained earnings; 4. participate; 5. premium, discount

Solved Problem

Solved Problem 17.1 Two separate business organizations, a partnership and a corporation, were formed on January 1, 2001.

1. The initial investments of the partners, Blue and Gray, were $25,000 and $20,000, respectively.

2. The Green Corporation has five stockholders, each owning 90 shares of $100-par common stock.

At the end of the calendar year, the net income of each company was $15,000. (a) For each organization, show the proper entry to close the Income Summary account. (b) Prepare a capital statement for the partnership and a stockholders' equity statement for the corporation, as of December 31, 2001.

Solution:

(a) Partnership Entry:

Income Summary	15,000	
Blue, Capital		7,500
Gray, Capital		7,500

Corporation Entry:

Income Summary	15,000	
Retained Earnings		15,000

(b) Partnership Capital Statement

	Blue	Gray	Total
Capital, 1/1/01	25,000	20,000	45,000
Add: Net Income	7,500	7,500	15,000
Capital, 12/31/01	32,500	27,500	60,000

Stockholders' Equity Statement

Common Stock $100 par	45,000
(450 shares authorized and issued)	
Retained Earnings	15,000
Stockholders' Equity	60,000

Index